THE KABALA OF NUMBERS

BOOK TWO

A Handbook of Interpretation

By Sepharial

New Edition
Enlarged and Revised

THE BOOK TREE
San Diego, California

Originally published
1913
McKay Publishing

New material & revisions
© 2010
The Book Tree
All rights reserved

ISBN 978-1-58509-337-3

Cover layout
Atulya Berube

Published by
The Book Tree
P O Box 16476
San Diego, CA 92176
www.thebooktree.com

We provide fascinating and educational products to help awaken the public to new ideas and
information that would not be available otherwise.
Call 1 (800) 700-8733 for our *FREE BOOK TREE CATALOG*.

CONTENTS   PART II

THE
KABALA OF NUMBERS
PART II

INTRODUCTION

THE increasing interest taken in the study of
numerical ratios and the occult significance of
numbers has created a growing demand for instruc-
tive works on the subject. Consequently, I have
undertaken a further and somewhat more complete
exposition in the present work, which may be
regarded as an extension and elaboration of the
principles of Numerology laid down in my first
volume bearing the same title. Unfortunately,
that book was hurried through press and contains
some errors which have already been noticed.
These were chiefly typographic errors, but there is
one of authorship which certainly requires explanation. Reference to the volume will show that I
have given three distinct systems of evaluation of
letters, namely : the Hebraic, the Pythagorean, and
the Phonetic or Universal. The idea in my mind
was to present each system on its own merits and
to illustrate each with some interpretations. This

1

was accordingly done, and a note of warning was given to the reader regarding the necessity of interpreting by the key belonging to the system from which the evaluation of the name was made. Thus, if the Hebraic values were used, the interpretation should be by means of the Tarot keys. If the Pythagorean values are used, the key given on p. 32 *et seq.*, which belongs to the Pythagorean system, should be used. Similarly, if the Universal alphabet is used for evaluation of a name, then the Planetary Key (pp. 45–46) is used for interpretation. Many readers, and even reviewers who should be above suspicion, have shown that they use one method of evaluation and various methods of interpretation, thus making nonsense of the whole process. They serve, however, to point out my error of authorship, which consists in giving various methods and keys in the same work. If I repeat the process in these pages, it will be with the express intention of showing that, properly worked, the methods are not in conflict but in agreement, and that each presents some aspect of the truth. Personally, I find the fullest satisfaction in the use of the Universal or Phonetic system of evaluation and the corresponding Planetary Key of Interpretation. This I have more fully developed in my *Cosmic Symbolism*, which was intended to be supplementary to the *Kabala*, pt. i., but has been found by many readers, unacquainted with astrology, to be too far advanced. So here, in these pages, I intend to give some new material on lines that are sufficiently plain to avoid all possibility of confusion, and it is believed that in following them the reader will find much that is of interest and not a little that may be rendered profitable study. My sole object in writing is to stimulate the public interest in the symbolism of numbers, and to suggest a certain necessary connection between our apprehension of things as facts of experience and the cosmic laws which underlie those facts.

I have already shown that cosmic laws are in operation whether we are conscious of them or not, and that their significance in human life, and possible utility for us, commence the moment we begin to apprehend those laws. For just as by an understanding of the forces of Nature man has been enabled to harness them to his use, so by an understanding of the laws governing the action of those forces, he may gain some further and more permanent advantage by intelligent co-operation. All the trouble in this world arises from the mistaken idea that we are surrounded by and invested with forces which have to be resisted and overcome. If, in the process, we come by any hurt, we invent a word to stand for our unconscious ignorance of natural laws, and promptly we speak of evil and the personification of evil. It is quite otherwise, however, when we happen to be going with the stream. Only the truly wise can regulate their desires and actions so as to be wholly in accord with Nature and the will of Heaven as expressed in natural laws. But all can to some extent regulate their goings and comings so as not to be in open conflict with their immediate environment, and to this end the study of the quantitive relations of things and persons, as expressed in sound, number, form, and colour, will greatly aid in the process of adaptation, by which alone security is assured to us. Adaptability to environment may, indeed, be said to be the secret of progress, success, happiness, and longevity. It represents the line of least resistance and that of greatest progress ; and it is only when we fail to adapt ourselves to our cosmic and social environment that pain and unhappiness are capable of assailing us. What we call adaptability on the physical plane finds its counterpart on the mental plane in elasticity. It is that quality of the mind which enables us to take an interest in the trivial things of life while engaging in the study of its deepest problems. It is, in a word, sympathy, the power of feeling and thinking with others, that is the sign of the most perfect sanity ; and as cause to effect, so sympathy moves us to adaptability. It is this flexibility, this roundness of temperament, that constitutes mental and physical well-being and fitness. To be wisely sympathetic would therefore appear most desirable, since it is in harmony, symmetry, and fitness that we attain the standards of goodness, beauty, and truth comprised in the triology of Plato's most desirable things. The perfect man is symmetrical, and it is by the study of our Greater Environment, of the laws that govern the universe in which we live, and of ourselves in relation thereto, that we may attain that symmetry of being which is competent for all occasions,— sympathetic, flexible, versatile, adaptable, fit.

This much for the benefit of my critic who found the *Kabala* so interesting that he regretted its application to horse-racing and similar popular speculations. For it is my purpose to further offend his susceptibilities and to assail his solitary position by fuller demonstration of facts pertaining to matters of common interest, and which are of interest solely because they are of human origin. To show that these are governed by law is to demonstrate the existence of a law of mind by which we come into relations with them and apprehend them as facts of our consciousness. It is my intention to show that the man who follows these things with an intelligent grasp of the laws that govern them is better equipped to come out successfully than one who operates in ignorance of those laws. From this as a basis of common interest and recognition it will then be possible to proceed to higher and more universal matters, but the man who would reach up to Heaven must have one end of his ladder firmly planted in his mother earth. So let us be sympathetic in matters that are commonplace, and comprehensive of that which is trivial. In such spirit I commend these pages to all and sundry in the belief that what I have written will prove useful.

SEPHARIAL.

LONDON, 1913.

CHAPTER I

THE NUMERICAL IDEA

To trace the development of the numerical idea in human thought would entail too deep a study for a work of this nature, and indeed I cannot lay claim to that encyclopædic knowledge which would be required to render such a study at all complete. It is, however, a matter of common knowledge that the development of the numerical idea was preceded by an instinctive perception of quantitive relations or ratios. Among aborigines we find no suspicion of mathematics and no nearer sense of actual values than is imported by the common needs of their existence; economics are an instinct with them, and, like the chimpanzee, they know "how many beans make five," but not six. In other words, they have the numerical idea in germ only, and it is expressed by crude generalities. They take comfort in numbers without any true sense of their working value; but civilisation, with a howitzer and a wireless detonator, judges two men to be better than a tribe. Quality begins to attach itself to number as soon as the primitive man is forced into the paths of civilisation. The primitive idea is persistent in the man who does not care what he eats so long as he gets enough. He is on the same mark as the aborigine who is father of ten children and owner of twenty kine, all very poor stuff, and knows not to discern that Kitmagū in the next hut is a better man than he with only two stalwart sons and three kine, all sound in wind and limb. But quantity and quality are jostling one another along our marts and boulevards wherever we may go. I have even heard a Rockefeller and a Vanderbilt envied by a man who ate four good meals every day and slept soundly for eight hours every night, and he, too, a man who really occupied more space at any one time than an average two! Now, what could a millionaire do more than he? True, he might commission any amount of labour, but he could not do the work, nor produce more than one man in one day. Economically he is not more effective nor more necessary to society than the scavenger, but he would not like you to say so. From a certain point of view your millionaire is a man who has gone a long way ahead of his fellows without making any real progress. If to the wealth of a Crœsus one could add the wisdom of a Solomon, and the compassion of a Sakyamuni, and the strength of a Milo, and the endurance of a Job, something symmetrical could be made of your plutocrat. At present he is only a man with a hump.

One can imagine, too, how the primitive man got hold of his idea of simple numbers as being invested with some strange significance—an occultism that

perhaps only the medicine-man of his tribe had any
notion of. For, to be sure, he had his lucky and
unlucky numbers, and he counted them out in
favour of his friends or against his enemies on the
bark of trees and on flat stakes and on the smooth
surface of the time-worn rocks. He made so many
straight strokes in imitation of rods or spears, and
lo ! the magic had been wrought ! He counted to
ten on his fingers or digits, and began a new series on
the thumb of the left hand because it was there he
began his count of One, coming as it did easiest to
the index finger of his right. So eleven was " ten
and one," and twenty-one was " twain-ten and one,"
and none can say what tale of sheep and oxen was
counted on that distinguished digit, the first that
man ever put a number to.

Counting by rods or sticks led no doubt to the
earliest geometrical relations of human thought.
One stick would represent existence, a fact or a thing
of man's perception, maybe a woman or a child, an
ox, a sheep, a flint-head, a day or a night. Two,
then, would stand for relative existence, and would
give use to the faculty of comparison, as by one being
longer and shorter than the other, thicker or thinner,
and thus heavier or lighter, stiffer or more supple.
What a great deal man began to know when he
counted two ! Yet not at once could he say by
how much one rod differed from the other, for
standards of measurement would come later. It
was just the fact that one rod stood for him and
another for the woman, his mate ; one for the boy
he had by her, the other for the girl he hoped to

have. The idea was a full one for the moment. Could he not bind those two sticks together with the thread of destiny snatched from the pampas grass or the water-weed ? Things were thus as they should be ; and when he came to examine all their relations, he found he could bring their tips together so as to form an inverted Λ, and thus was evolved the first symbol of humanity—the creature with two sides, a male and a female, one that is supple and one that is strong. But he could not enclose a space between them, and this suggested an incompleteness and gave rise to a new idea, and the number Three was born in the human mind. By placing the divided ends of his two sticks upon the ground he could remedy their incompleteness by giving them a solid base on which to rest, so the Earth was called Son, child of the Father-Mother, by name Tu. Now this was a perfect thing—Father, Mother, and Child ; and its perfection was made manifest under an everlasting symbol when the man walked around the woman, and a circle, of which she was the centre, was inscribed on the ground ⊙. The idea was one that fastened upon the primitive mind, and the number three was henceforth invested with a special significance, altogether wonderful, magical, divine. Then, of course, the three greatest things in Nature answered at once to the native thought—the Sun as father, the Moon as mother, and the Earth as son ; and thus they have persisted through the religions of nations, in no form more familiar or less obscured by lapse of time and traditional imposts than in the trinity of the

Egyptians, known as Osiris, Isis, and Horus. Thus the story of three sticks, of the magic tripod, the fortunate triangle, and the lucky three that has universal currency.

Here are the forms which presented themselves to the wild man of the woods as he played with three sticks :—

They are all primitive forms that have persisted in various of the world's scripts—Greek, Coptic, Moabite, Chinese, Latin, English,—and every one of them invested with a magical significance as primitive as the forms themselves. Look at that Delta. Who does not know it for a lucky triangle, with the child-stick lying supine at the feet of the happy parents united above? And that other triangle where the base line is uppermost and the heads of the family debased. That surely is a symbol of evil, and so indeed we find it in all the symbolism of the Hermetists, the Kabalists, and the Rosicrucians.

From the same three sticks we get the variant forms of the letter A in three different countries, the universal symbol of the Star and the Chinese symbol of Heaven. With his circle before him, suggesting the round of a tree, and his three sticks in hand, the camp-stool would soon be evolved. Home was already in sight, and soon the round sherd, supported by three sticks over a fire, would be bubbling over with the good things of the earth. Truly the number three was a lucky one !

Four, of course, was bound to follow ; for it was the number of realisation and materiality, the symbol of possession (*Kab.*, i. 46). The quadrate idea first took definite form when man began to parcel out the land and peg his claim. Four rods would enclose a space convenient for allotment. Contiguous circles would leave blank spaces in between. So four came to be associated with possession in territory, things solid and material on which the primitive idea could take a firm stand. You will find it in the earliest hieroglyphs used in this connection and continued in the records of past civilisations. In ancient Chinese character it is a circle with a cross inside ; and the same form is found in the Egyptian hieroglyphs, standing for territory. Without the cross it appears as a square form, signifying an enclosure, a field or plot of land —*tien*. Astronomically it is used as the symbol of the Earth. These are traditional values of symbols invented by our early progenitors, and they have persisted because they are natural correspondences.

In process of time calculation led to multiplication by addition, and division by subtraction, to an appreciation of fractional parts, proportional values, etc., and thus to the institution of standards of measurement. Life soon became a serious business, and Numbers a Council of Perfection.

In the case of Meum *v.* Tuum the Court first of all impanelled a jury of ten—five men and five women. The women were afterwards expunged, leaving a *panchayat.* It was a one-handed business, with plenty of prejudice at the back of it; and when seven eggs had to be split between man and wife, or brother and sister, it always happened that the man got four and the woman three. Man's sense of equity obscured the finding of the jury, and the formula $\frac{7}{2} = \frac{4+3}{2}$ constitutes perhaps one of the most intricate problems that have been handed down to us from antiquity. Hence it is that the $4+3$ formula has come to be a bone of contention, some saying that the half of seven is three and a half, while others affirm that you cannot split seven eggs anyhow without making a lot of mess and trouble. The conventicle known as the W.S.P.U. has taken the problem seriously in hand, and probably we shall hear more of it in the near future. In the polity of nations it was not long before the Council of Twelve became a permanent institution, and the duodecimal system was applied to the world's business. Lately, however, there has been a tendency to revert to Nature's original simplicity, and counting by tens has found advocates wherever numbers are largely dealt with. In the ancient use of the Calculus—the coloured shells are still in use among the astronomers of Southern India—the decimal system was followed. Zero was represented by a coloured shell, and the numbers 1 to 9 by plain shells in a row. Ten began the second row with a shell of a different colour, and was followed by nine plain ones. Thus continuously the digits were ranged in ten rows of nine, and the power was

prefixed to each line by a coloured or marked
indicator, the form being

	0	1	2	3	4	5	6	7	8	9
1	0	1	2	3	4	5	6	7	8	9
2	0	1	2	3	4	5	6	7	8	9
3	0	1	2	3	4	5	6	7	8	9
4	0	1	2	3	4	5	6	7	8	9
5	0	1	2	3	4	5	6	7	8	9
6	0	1	2	3	4	5	6	7	8	9
7	0	1	2	3	4	5	6	7	8	9
8	0	1	2	3	4	5	6	7	8	9
9	0	1	2	3	4	5	6	7	8	9
10	0	1	2	3	4	5	6	7	8	9

and this could be raised indefinitely by shifting the
power line by the addition of a vertical line to the
right. I have seen very elaborate calculations
performed in a few minutes by expert calculators,
and I remember to have begun a kindergarten
course of study with something of the same kind,
coloured balls running on horizontal wires set in a
framework of wood ; but I do not remember to have
arrived at any stupendous results, the machine
serving principally as a weapon of assault upon
those who disputed my calculations, or otherwise
disturbed my peace.

It is difficult indeed to show any but traditional
authority for the idea that numbers carry with them
a specific meaning. The key to the position seems
to lie in the association of the number Nine with
Vulcan, he who binds and looses, and thus with the
Demiurgos the creative agent or Logos of the present

race of humanity, associated in mythology with both the principle of Good and that of Evil. Man thus numerically symbolised is the universal solvent, the maker and fulfiller of his own destiny, himself the problem and the calculator, the propounder and resolver of all questions. And here it is well to note that the questions that vex us are not universal ones, the Great Artificer has the finished work already in hand. Our race is not the first humanity to which the earth has served as seeding-ground. This seminary of Heaven has already yielded many crops. The problem of existence is solely and entirely ours, and it is for us to solve it—suitably by continued existence, for it is probably a true saying that " Life is a riddle that resolves itself." Vulcan, the forger of those chains that bind humanity to the rock of necessity, is thus seen to be Humanity itself. Thus Arnold in *The Light of Asia*, bk. viii. :

> " Ho ! ye suffer from yourselves, none else compels ;
> None other holds you that you lag and stay,
> And whirl upon the Wheel, and hug and kiss
> Its spokes of agony, its tyre of tears,
> Its nave of nothingness ! "

The number Nine as Vulcan, as Humanity, comes therefore to be symbolical of Karma, the law of retributive justice, action and reaction, the compelling force of necessity, the power of an infinite freedom. It is associated with the planet Mars (*Kab.*, i. 46, 59, etc.) and the colour red, the symbol of desire.

Now, desire is at the root of all action, and is the

fire that, acting on the fluidic body, is responsible for all forms of emotion. Working on the mental plane it produces the flame of intelligence, the flash of genius, and the will-to-do in every department of mental activity. It is the " colour " principle in the human soul, as intelligence is the "form" principle. It corresponds to heat, as intelligence to light. Without this desire-principle life would be inanimate and colourless, a valley of shadows, an Acheron. Desire it is that binds us and desire that sets us free.

Number Nine therefore has that magic in it that the Kabalists have identified it with the " Red Dragon " of Alchemy, the Universal Solvent, and the only means of transmutation. We cannot count higher than nine without falling into zero and beginning a new gamut. That and 0 are the beginning and end of existence, the Alpha and Omega of human possibility. On other planes the power is raised ; but the limitation would appear to be the same. Hence nine is symbolical of the limit of conscious activity ; zero the womb from which all life emanates and into which it all returns.

If we inquire as to the cause of this limitation of the mind by which we are compelled to count in terms of nine, we shall probably come to the conclusion that certain fixed laws of thought are imposed upon us by reason of our production from, and existence in, a world that is founded upon the cube of three. Our distance-sensation, which by continuity gives us the idea of space, is limited in three directions : as by length, breadth, and thickness. Our duration-

sensation, from which we derive the abstract idea
of Time, is also limited in three directions: as by
past, present, and future.   Our sensations of duration and distance are linked together by our
perception of correlated succession—as, for instance,
that bodies are in continuous juxtaposition in all
directions of the same plane, and that events are
consecutive in similar manner.   It is only when we
pierce through successive planes—as physical,
sensory, emotional, mental, and spiritual—that we
emerge upon the abstract ideas of Space and Time,
and find that they are one and the same, being, in
fact, linked together as concepts of the mind in the
consciousness of our continued existence.   The
correlated succession of mental phenomena is as
much a fact in psychology as is that of physical
phenomena in physics.   If we regard incarnation,
apart from its duration, as a single act, it will be
possible to relate it at once to a past cause and a
future effect.   The actor becomes a necessary
permanent factor, and his embodied existence in
this world but the consequence of a past life and
the cause of that which is to be.

But I am getting side-tracked in the long grass,
and must return to the idea of numbers.

It would necessarily follow from the consideration
that a certain numerical law governs all phenomenal
sequence, that men would acquire the belief that
particular numbers have a fortunate significance
and others one that is sinister.   One of the earliest
conceptions in this direction was that founded upon
the traditional belief that man was first created,

and afterwards woman. Then 1 would represent Adam or other first of a particular race, and 2 would be the symbol of Eve or other first of mothers. So numbers were alternately male and female, the odd numbers being male and the even female. Perhaps that is why Oddfellows and others of the male persuasion affirm "there is luck in odd numbers," and why also their best Seconds have sworn to be " even " with them.

In process of time, by observation of events of happy or sinister nature in connection with certain dates, days, numbers, etc., all the digits would acquire a traditional significance. Such a significance appears to have attached to the numbers 3, 7, 12, and multiples of these, in all theologies. The Masonic symbol of the eye within the triangle as the emblem of the Deity, has its counterpart in the Hebraic Yod with the triangle, and the Kabalistic talisman of the ten yods forming a triangle thus :

By a number of deft manipulations of figures the Rabbinical experts were able to, read an entirely new and mystical meaning into the Hebrew Scripture, and this they embodied in a work which was called *Zohar*. But whereas they made use of three distinct forms of computation, they were faithful to

2

the text and to the traditional values of the Hebrew
letters, and also to their methods, so that it is
surprising they should have evolved so perfect a
system.   Indeed it is open to us to believe either
that the author or authors of the Scriptures deliberately planned the glyph and communicated
the key to the Kabala, or that the writing of the
Scripture was effected under the operation of the
Law of Mind, which finds its interpretation in the
mystical science of numbers ; and I have already
shown that such a Kabalism was imposed by the
ancients upon cosmical phenomena, or that, alternatively, cosmic symbolism gave rise to the methods
of the Kabalists.   That they are in singular
agreement none will dispute who have made any
patient study of the subject (see *Cosmic Symbolism*).

Having given a permanent value to the letters of
the alphabet, the consistent Kabalist proceeded by
three methods to give a new value to every word or
group of letters, and thus a new meaning to every
sentence.   By the *Notaricon* method he extracted
the letters from the beginnings of words, from the
ends of words, and by a regular sequence thus
obtained certain letters which, being brought
together and divided into words, gave a new sentence that was not only intelligible in itself, but
apposite to the purport of the text from which it
was drawn.   By *Gemetria* he gave a value to each
letter in a word and then reduced the whole word to
its unit value, dealing thus successively with the
words of the text, so that finally he had a number of

figures which, being converted into letters, gave an oracular key to the meaning of the text. By *Temurah* he changed the letters of the text by the application of certain set rules embodied in the Table of Tziruph, so that a new interpretation of the text was open to him. Illustrations of these three methods will be found in *The Manual of Occultism*. I have no part in the Bacon-Shakespeare controversy, but I am prepared to show that whoever wrote the plays was a Rosicrucian and Kabalist, and an expert in the use of Kabalistic keys. For not only does he extract a truth from the symbolism of Nature and embody it in his text, but he hides a truth in the text and gives you the key in the symbol. Also, he makes use of recondite points familiar only to versed astrologers and students of alchemical literature. We cannot deny that all things are possible to genius, since it works by inspiration; but it is more reasonable to suppose that in a studied cryptogram of this nature, conscious purpose was the moving power and experience the chief agent. The author, however, had many models upon which to frame his cryptic sentences, for secret writing of this sort had long been in use during times of wars and insurrection, and Kabalists continually use such means of conveying their teachings to those who are keen enough to perceive that an obscure sentence contains its own elucidation. Sometimes a signal is given, as by some typographic error, peculiar spelling, or the use of an ambiguous word. The writings of Nostradamus are full of such signals, cryptograms, and anagrams.

Shakespeare abounds with them. In the *Exodus* there are three consecutive verses, each consisting of seventy-two letters, which are used for conveying the names of the Seventy-two Principalities known to Kabalists as the *Shemhamphorœ*, and they are each set over the gates of the temple, six at each gate, and three gates upon each side—one facing north, another south, one east, and another west. Astrologers similarly divide the celestial circle into four quadrants, of three signs each, answering to the four quarters of the heavens; and each sign is again divided into three decans of 10° each, and these are split into two of 5° each, so that in all there are 4 × 3 × 3 × 2, or 72 "faces," as they are called, and each carries its own description and characteristics.

When, finally, in the evolution of the numerical idea, we come to the study of physics, philosophy, and even art, we find they are all capable of a mathematical and geometrical statement, and indeed there are some abstract ideas which cannot otherwise be communicated but by geometrical symbols and mathematical formulæ. So much is this method in vogue that it has been said that nothing is to be regarded as fact which does not admit of a mathematical statement, and yet we find that all the higher sciences make free use of symbols and formulæ in connection with them which have no existence as facts in Nature, but are merely relative truths. It would be interesting, for instance, to see a mathematical statement of the real motion in space of a body which moves in an elliptical orbit about another body occupying one of the foci, which itself moves in an elliptical orbit about a third body. This would be the moon's actual path in space as seen from a stationary sun.

But Kabalism is not concerned with such complexities. Rather it seeks to define the Universe as Symbol in terms of fixed values which have direct relation to the nature and constitution of man. Thus, although it makes use of the parabola, the hyperbola, and ellipsis, it regards man as a fixed centre of consciousness, to which all phenomena are related by a law of correspondence; himself embodied universe in a universe that is himself, with numbers as the only key to the understanding of its mysteries.

CHAPTER II

THE GEOMETRY OF NATURE

HINTON says in one of his books on the Fourth Dimension : " We know a great deal about the How of things but little or nothing about the Why." Nearer the truth, we may affirm that we know very little of either. But what we do know is enough to give a balance in favour of Hinton's conclusion. We know how water crystallises ; we can make ice. We know it crystallises always at an angle of 60°. But why ? This beats us. We know the various angles at which the metals crystallise, but our science does not enable us to say why they preserve these angles. It only enables us to recognise them. We have learned, in fact, a great deal of the physiognomy of Nature, but little or nothing of its soul, of the intelligence that lies behind its myriad marvels. Of Nature's geometry we have learned somewhat ; of the Geometer we know nothing but what is expressed in the work. " Looking through Nature " is therefore the only sane way of regarding any truths presented as religion. If we steadily regard the geometry of Nature in the same patient and sincere manner as did Hipparchus, Ptolemy, Kepler, Tycho, Newton, Kelvin, and others we shall probably come to the conclusion that number, as expressed in geometrical relations, is the most intimate expression of the Soul of things. Doubtless in the aggregate they seem to be endowed with more obvious qualities, which impress us in a more superficial way, as when we observe how beautiful, how grand and strong is Nature, how persistent and enduring. But closer study will show that these qualities are facts of our consciousness, that the standards of beauty and strength are ours, and that what underlies all natural phenomena is the geometry of things expressed by definite quantitive relations. Let these relations be disturbed by even a little and Nature breaks forth in fierce protest, flashing with the lightning of her eyes from beneath lowering brows, and calling with a thousand-voiced thunder across the dark abysm of night for speedy restitution.

And our study of this geometry has enabled us to understand and predict her moods, and even to utilise her magnificent strength in a multitude of ways. It was that supreme genius John Kepler who first defined for us the relations of the various bodies in our immediate universe. What are known as Kepler's Laws, which were later demonstrated by Newton, are the first and fullest expression of the principles of cosmology. They reveal to us a geometry from which there is no escape, and anybody bold enough to deny the intelligence underlying them must be prepared to explain in a manner satisfactory to the scientific mind why these laws apply throughout the universe.   And this is imperative, despite the fact that Science frequently makes use of a term for which it has no certain explanation or final definition.   As an instance, I may cite the attraction of gravitation as one of the big labels concealing an empty bottle.   For many years it has been tucked away on a dark shelf, nobody having any special concoction with which to fill it.

Kepler's Laws may here be enumerated.   The first is that the planets in their motion round the Sun describe equal areas in equal times.   If a line be imagined as joining the Sun with each of the planets at their several distances, then these lines or vectors will, in the same period of time, enclose triangles whose areas are all equal.   Hence it follows that the nearer a planet is to the Sun the greater must be its velocity.   From this proposition was derived the second, namely, if the distance of a planet from the Sun is variable so must its velocity be.

The second law is that the planets describe ellipses round the Sun, which occupies one of the foci. From this Newton derived his theory of gravitation, by which it was required that the planets were urged towards the Sun by a force inversely as the squares of their distances.   The said "force" was called gravitation—a term that, as I have said, covers a great deal but conveys nothing.   For Kepler's law was only true in relation to a stationary sun ; and when, as would inevitably follow from the universal application of the law of evolution, it

was discovered and proved by observation that the
Sun was not and never has been stationary in
space, but was continually pursuing an orbit of its
own, it was seen that the elliptical orbit could not
be a fact in Nature, but was the expression of a
relative truth only.

To illustrate this, let it be said a man on board
ship walks in an ellipse around a mast. If his
course were traced it would be found that, in
relation to the mast, his course was elliptical, and
would represent the orbit of Kepler's planet. And
let it be supposed that the mast exerts a magnetic
attraction on the man, constant in all directions.
Now, since the mast would be in one of the foci of
the ellipse, it would be necessary that, as he ap-
proached the mast in his elliptical path, he would
have to accelerate his motion in order to resist
being drawn into collision with the mast, since
motion is our only means of overcoming the force
we call gravitation. And to compensate for this
hurried transit he might go slower when, at the
greater distance, he was further from the centre of
attraction. This is a crude illustration of Kepler's
law and Newton's conclusion therefrom.

Now, of course, it will be said at once that inasmuch
as the mast moves with the ship, it is possible to
describe an ellipse around a moving body. In
reference to the relations of the man and the mast
it is so, but from the point of view of a spectator
outside the ship it is not so. For let the man start
on his orbital journey at the moment he is in line
with the mast on board and the spectator beyond

on the wharf. By the time he has completed his
course and come again to the place on deck from
which he started out, it will be seen that he is no
longer in line with the mast and spectator, but
many yards or miles away, according to the relative
velocities of himself and the ship. Therefore his
true motion in space cannot be an ellipse at all,
neither is it a cycloid, since this infers that the body
revolving round a centre in motion shall maintain
the same relations with that centre. An ellipse
infers that these relations shall be continually
variable. Kepler therefore apprehended and formu-
lated a relative truth only, while Newton based
his theory upon it as if it were a fact. Both these
great minds, however, brought us into intelligent
relations with our greater environment and gave us
a convenient point of view from which to study the
geometry of Nature. Kepler's third law is that the
centripetal (attractive) force varies inversely as the
square of the distance, for any one or for all planets.
From this we may conclude that the squares of the
periodic times are to each other as the cubes of the
mean distances of the planets. This is the converse
statement of the same relative fact. Anciently it
was thought that the relations of the bodies of the
system were constant. Modern observations compared with ancient ones suggest that they are
variable. The equilibrium of the universe is found
to be unstable and in a continual state of adjustment.
The universe is in a state of flux. For aught we
know there may come a time when the relations of
the bodies in a system become constant, but it is

xtremely improbable from our present point of view.
Bruno evidently thought it so when he said : " Infinite variability is the eternal juvenescence of God."

From the fact that it is possible to calculate the
places of the Sun, Moon, and planets for centuries
in advance, we may perceive that the geometry
of Nature is a fact upon which we may certainly
depend with considerable security. This is the
telescopic point of view. When we turn to the
microscopic and examine her features in miniature,
we find the same consistency, the same stability.
The characteristics of a particle of iron, or of any
kind of stone, or vegetable form are the same to-day
as they were thousands of years ago. We recognise things by their features. The physiognomy
of Nature is not evasive. It is an interesting fact
that the superior metals crystallise at the angle
or complemental angle of a regular polygon. If
they sometimes followed one form and sometimes
another we should not recognise them for what they
are. We depend for the fidelity of our perceptions
upon the integrity of the Great Geometer.

The fact that He never fails us has indeed led the
superficial to presume that He never can, and that
there is a blind mechanical law at work in the
world by which things must inevitably continue as
they are and always have been. " It always was and
always will be " is the stock phrase of the frying-
pan intellect. More depth and rotundity of mind
would enable him at least to see that God is under
no contract with us to complete His work. The
maker of images may destroy his moulds. All the

great world-teachers have laid stress upon the
doctrine of Conditional Immortality, the condition
being obedience to the spiritual law. For aught we
know the physical stability of the universe is conditional too. Modern research would seem to
indicate that post-mortem existence is an assured
fact. But whereas we may have undeniable
testimony of survival of bodily death in some
instances, it has not been shown that even this is a
universal fact. And between post-mortem existence or continuity of personal life and immortality
there is a great gulf fixed. But this we know for a
fact, that in order to produce a chemical effect we
have to supply certain chemical conditions, and the
same may be said of electrical effects ; and if we are
disposed to regard physical existence as due to
chemical or electrical energy, we know that its
continuance depends on the maintenance of the
necessary conditions. If a personality can go to
pieces through a disturbance of the equilibrium of
its forces, why not a universe ? Indeed we have
before us, in the space between the orbits of Mars
and Jupiter, an illustration of a disrupted planet.
In the sudden flaring up of the star Nova Persei we
probably have sight of the disruption of a solar
system. Cities have been swept away, continents
submerged, valleys thrown up to the mountains,
mountains cast into the sea, planets and stars
exploded in space. Who is daring enough to affirm
the stability of the solar system ?'

But while it continues to exist it will follow the
same cosmic, electrical, chemical, and dynamic

laws as have operated from the beginning. Why ?
Because, as Plato says, " God geometrises," and
these laws, which we apprehend and call physical,
are the numerical and geometrical expressions of
that Intelligence which constructed, animates, and
invests the physical universe.

> " We are but parts of one stupendous whole,
> Whose body Nature is, and God the Soul ! "

Providing we extend our ideas of Nature to include the whole telescopic universe, allowing that
what is perceived by us is probably but an infini-
tesimal part of the possibly perceptible, and what we
know of it certainly but the smallest fraction of
what is possibly knowable, we may read into these
lines, simple as they are, the most profound philosophical and religious belief that ever inspired the
mind of man. Neither Pythagoras, nor Plato, nor
Kepler, nor Bruno taught anything that differed
from it, or was ever more profoundly true. All
these had communed with Nature and had caught
some whisperings of the Voice of the Silence, but
who can say that any had entered into her secret
counsel or knew anything of the purpose of creation
—of the why and wherefore of existence ? As
vessels made to honour, and bearing the inscription,
"צדק ליהוה," they carry each their quota of the water
of life, which is for the healing of the nations.
But the virtue of communion is not in the wafer or
the wine, but in the attitude of the communicant.
It is for us to study the language of Nature in a
proper spirit, if we would learn to read its symbols

and gain any practical knowledge of its secret operations.   And the key to this study is Numbers —ratios, quantitive relations, the geometry of things.   But whereas it has become the fashion of our philosophers to state their arguments and conclusions in complex mathematical formulæ, making of mathematics a recondite and cryptic language that he who runs may not read, being, in fact, in too much of a hurry to understand anything but plain English, the ancient philosophers were more conservative in the use of numbers, which they used in a symbolical sense.   If it be true, as it doubtless is, that nothing can be accepted as fact which does not admit of a mathematical statement —though I have tried unsuccessfully to reduce a jumping toothache to terms of x,—it is equally true that nothing is capable of a mathematical statement which cannot be expressed in plain English, and that with less chance of being misunderstood.

That quaint mystical philosopher Jacob Boehme makes use of Numbers only in a mystical sense, and he is worth studying.   Eckhartshausen uses them in a symbolical sense.   Cagliostro, that genius whom most writers have mistaken for a mountebank, used them in a Kabalistic sense.   It is in this latter that they come to have a practical value.   Of all Numerologists he is the only one who has shown anything to justify his teachings, and the fact that he accidentally ran into the tail-end of the Holy Inquisition only goes to show that the Church did not know how to tackle the business end of a proposition.   With a proper sense of the fitness of things they would have given him a cardinal's cap, and left it to his artistic sense to fill the part and to his sense of gratitude to fill the coffers. I am a great advocate of Laotze's doctrine that everything exists for a purpose and that the virtue of everything is in its use. Hence I would make generals of all our bandits and admirals of all our pirates, providing they had given us enough trouble to qualify for the posts. For, after all, there is only one man who can do anything well, and that is he who knows the business. On the same principle, I think that if there is any practical good in a thing, it is good to be known. Your average esotericist would cut all his cake in a dark corner. I am well assured that there is only one cure for a hungry man, and that is a square meal of something fit to eat. Previous experience along these occult lines of study has shown me that only those who are ready for the idea can apprehend and absorb it. A good many can digest it, being of the educated-ostrich type of mind, keen on anything that means new knowledge, and punctual at meal times. But very few assimilate it. It does not enter into their constitution and become a part of themselves. It fails to affect their beliefs and their view-point in life. It is an adjunct, not a component of their mental being. Knowing this, one does not overfeed them nor put all the good things on the table at once.

Now, the connection of all this with the geometry of Nature may appear remote, but it is not really so. I have sought to show by citation of the

conclusions of great observers and thinkers tha
Nature has a geometry and that it is intelligible
only because and inasmuch as it expresses an
Intelligence. Doubtless we must finally conclude
that the geometric sense is vested in us, otherwise
we could not apprehend the geometrical. It is a
certain truth that our powers of apprehension are
limited to those things the principles of whose
existence are within ourselves. Does, anybody
think the rose is conscious of its own beauty and
blushes because we admire it ? It is we who define
our own standards of beauty, of goodness, of truth.
We are conscious of these things in proportion as
they are active principles of our own minds. They
are apprehended by the single sense of harmony.
Goodness is harmony, beauty is harmony, truth is
harmony. In what, then, consists our sense of
harmony ? It is inherent in the soul of man, in his
laws of thought, in the numerical constitution of
his being. According to his evolution and his
position in the scale of being, he embodies and
responds to a definite set of vibrations. He
apprehends number because he *is* number. The
mass-chord of all personal vibrations may be taken
as the man's physical constitution. The mass-
chord of all his emotional vibrations is the net
result of his psychic constitution. His thought-
vibrations are limited by his gamut of consciousness.
The average clodpole does not understand this fact,
but he can tell you something about pigs and
potatoes that are possibly worth knowing. He
does not understand why we are all invading his

beautiful Garden of Eden these summer days, but he has an eye to the fact that we have brought some money with us. He has lived fifty years in this Paradise on earth and knows not that it is beautiful, and that to be in it, if only for awhile, we are willing to pay the price of many months of labour! Yet he points with evident pride to that triumph of porcine culture, the crown of all his labours : " That there be a foine pig, look ye ! "

So, as Number is apprehended by us only because it is inherent in us as a principle of being, so our appreciation of it in Nature and in our daily life will be in proportion to the development in us of the numerical idea. The man of commerce thinks in pounds sterling, the wrestler and pugilist in pounds avoirdupois. The linguist thinks in words, the geometer in forms, the mathematician in numbers. The language we think and speak in, is the language of our individual natures, tastes, appetites, desires, and aspirations. We are an embodiment of cosmic vibrations, we make use of vibrations and produce them in others. But each of us has his dominant note, colour, number, or vibration, and answers to that note in others. Not that we are limited to sympathy only with those who are of the same character and governed by the same number, for each of us can reproduce those states of con- sciousness and those phases of emotion, desire, passion, etc., through which we have evolved ; but each of us has a basic note, a dominant which sounds through all the movements and variations of life's orchestration and adds its power of tone to

3

the universal harmony. This dominant characteristic or synthesis of characteristics can be
expressed as a colour or aura, by a geometrical
form, by a note, or by a number. It has been
referred to as a " signature " by Jacob Boehme in
his *Signatura Rerum,* and in this sense is a physiognomy imposed by Nature. Boehme further shows
these various types or signatures to be manifest
under Four Complexions, whereby he evolves in two
separate works a species of mystical astrology, as
if he had dealt with the planets in one book and the
four " elements " in the other. For clearly enough
he understood these four " complexions " or phrases
to be represented by the four Fixed Signs of the
Zodiac which enter into the composition of the
ancient symbols of the Assyrian Bull and the
Egyptian Sphinx, as well as the Hebrew Cherubim.
The Lion, Man, Eagle, and Bull are figures of the
four " elements " or states of Matter known to the
Kabalists as the spiritual, mental, psychic, and
physical. Two of them are light, namely, Leo and
Aquarius, the Lion and the Man, the Spirit and the
Mind ; and two are dark, the Eagle (Dragon) and the
Bull, the animal soul and body, represented by water
and earth, and the signs Scorpio and Taurus. Boehme
makes them correspond with the Four Seasons and
the four corners of the Earth or cardinal points.

So, then, if we take the nine digits as connected
with the planets (*Kab.,* i. 59–60), and consider that
these are represented on each of the four planes of
existence, then it may be that a man may be
numerically represented on the several successive

planes by the numbers 3, 5, 6, 9, making a composite
total of 23, which, being reduced to its unit value
=5, which brings him finally under the signature
of Mercury, the colour Indigo and the note E.

Thus any horoscope may be taken showing the
places of the planets in the signs, and the signs being
arranged according to the " elements," the values
attaching to each plane of activity may be totalled
and unified, so that in the end we may obtain the
" signature " or mass-chord of the man.   Suppose,
for example, we have a horoscope in which Saturn
is in Libra, Jupiter in Scorpio, Mars in Aquarius,
Venus in Aquarius, the Sun in Pisces, Mercury in
Pisces, and the Moon in Leo.   Here the Sun must be
taken as 4, being in a negative sign ; and the Moon as
7, being in a positive sign ; the other planets as
given in *Kab.*, i. 42.

The signs and planets involved are as follows :—

ΔFire   —Leo   Moon   .   .   .   7
=Air   —Libra—Aquarius.
            Saturn—Mars, Venus   . 8 9 6
∇Water —Pisces—Sun, Jupiter, Mer-
            cury 4 3 5
+Earth —Nil.

The unit values of these are :

Spiritual	7	unit value	=7
Mental	896 = 23	,,	=5
Psychic	435 = 12	,,	=3
Physical	0	,,	=0

Mass-chord   =15 = 6 Sig.

But inasmuch as Saturn and the other planets are all represented in the horoscope at whatsoever time it is struck, we have to modify their values according to the signs they are in, since the same coloured light shining through a differently coloured medium will appear differently. For this reason certain numbers are ascribed by the Kabalists to the twelve signs and gates of the heavens (see *Cosmic Symbolism*). The number of the planet and sign being then multiplied together and reduced to its unit value, the mass-chord will be different for each combination of planetary influences, and the resultant signature will be one of the nine digits. But a more convenient method of enumerating the planetary configurations is to multiply the planetary number by the number of the planet whose sign it occupies, and then to reduce it to a unit value. Those of my readers who are interested in numerical horoscopy will no doubt take the hint and follow it out to its proper conclusion. I have here sought only to indicate that the geometry of Nature finds expression in the individual solely because he is compounded of the cosmic elements and himself a reflex of all that he beholds. For if man looks into the mirror of Nature fairly and squarely, and not obliquely or with a mental squint, he will inevitably see only himself.

CHAPTER III

NUMBER AS EXPRESSING THOUGHT

THE idea of the Universe as Divine Ideation in expression of Form leads directly to the subject of human thought in relation to number, and of number as expressing thought.

If we regard thinking man individually as a centre of consciousness in the Divine Mind we shall logically proceed to argue his physical existence as corresponding with a cosmic brain-cell, and of his consequent subjugation to a Law of Mind imposed upon him by reason of this relativity. A man cannot think as he will. If he thinks at all, he thinks as he must. He is bridled and directed by the laws of his being. It is even logical to carry the argument to the Supreme Centre and say that God is what He is by reason of His deity. According to the laws of our thought He cannot transcend the Law of His Being. He must be good, being God. He must preserve that which He has created because it is the consistent continuance of His Divine thought. Without the physical universe He can have no bodily existence. The visible universe is the vestment of God.

The man, the subsidiary agent, is what he is by reason of a preordination, and every individual unit subserves some special function of the universal economy. He is subject to the laws governing the whole body to which he belongs ; he is obedient to the laws governing that organ of the organic whole of which he forms a subsidiary and integral part. Without his co-operation the economy of the universe is ineffectual. He is a cell in a brain centre. The Mind that animates him is supreme.

Taught by the experience of many incarnations to subserve the general economy of the particular function and organ to which he is related, he may even qualify for a higher function and consequent embodiment in a higher organ of the Divine Man. There is no limit to his perfectibility. He can evolve indefinitely until he reaches that supreme co-ordinating centre in the brain of the Grand Man in which resides the function of individual consciousness—the sense of the I am I,—to which all else is subsidiary.

Every individual, hence, responds to a particular number—the highest of which is Adam, אדם $= 144 = 9$ made in the "image and likeness of God." Now, God here is the Logos of our solar system, and it is not to be argued that the key number of our system is that of any other in the greater Universe. Suppose, for instance, that our solar system occupies the position of the right knee in the Grand Man—well, that is a long way from the brain, and yet so intimately linked up with it that any hurt or disturbance taking place in our system would be instantly known and provided for in the Supreme Centre.

And, according to Oriental teachings, in the *Guptavidyâ*, our humanity has not attained to a higher vibration than 5. We find man of this world blessed with five senses and five digits on foot and hand. It is a limitation imposed by correspondence, and the rest of this cycle of evolution will proceed along this fivefold line of development. Five is the number of Mercury, and its supreme function is the getting of knowledge. The quest of knowledge is therefore the key-note of our cycle. In all our Kabala we find a place for it in the centre of our scheme. In *Cosmic Symbolism* I have shown that it is the only number that is universally related and has no polarity, being itself the symbol of the co-ordinating centre of our material consciousness, *i.e.* the sensorium. All the five senses yield their impressions to the sensorium. The sum-total of our sense-impressions is experience. We are limited therefore to a fivefold apperception of things, and the development of a sixth sense lies in the experience thence derived. If now we regard all sensations as sets of vibrations, coming to us through atmosphere as sound, through light as colour, through privation of light as form, etc., then we shall come close to the perception of the numerical relations of thought. Our sense of harmony is bounded by a definite set of vibrations. We instinctively sense the fitness of certain sounds to express particular emotions. A military march,

for instance, requires the flamboyant key of G
major. To convey a sense of yearning or
regret we fall naturally into the minor. We flat
our music automatically to convey a sense of
depression.

Who taught us these things save Nature, working
through the senses. Perceive that my conception of
Nature transcends the senses. Nature does not
cease to exist where we cease to perceive her ! The
limitations of the senses are part of our environment.
We know that our sense of touch is related to solids,
or bodies that affect our muscular sense ; that taste
is related to fluids ; smell to vapours ; hearing to
atmospheres ; and sight to ether. Yet all these
senses are but forms of touch. Seeing, hearing,
smelling, and tasting are all effected by contact.
It is only a matter of vibration. There are things
we cannot see because they are so fine and ethereal
we have no nerves delicate enough to register their
contact. Below our sense of touch there may be
things so solid we cannot feel them. Things
outside the gamut of our sensations do not exist for
us. We live in a world of relativity, and our relations are extremely narrow and limited. The
rotifera and other infusoria find plenty of play-
space in a drop of water that has been squeezed
quite flat between two plates of glass. From the
point of view of an Universal Intelligence our solar
system may be a mere speck upon the glass, a
microscopic culture of quite second-rate interest.
It is a good thing that we are able to regard
ourselves microscopically. We thus get a better

sense of our true relations to the infinite universe
about us.

Seeing, then, that sensation follows a certain
growth or development from one grade of touch to
another that is finer, we may quite reasonably
suppose that in a future state of evolution mankind
will become possessed of yet finer faculties and
correspondingly finer organisms than at present
he possesses. Yet even in regard to those that we
have it is seen that there is a considerable range, and
only the educated sense, whether it be that of touch
or sight or any other, is capable of defining our
standards of perception.

The idea is that within this general fifth stage of
human development in the present cycle of humanity there are nine principal modulations. They are
sensory as to degree and mental as to expression.
The degree of individual development will determine the particular tastes, inclinations, and habits of
mind evinced by a man. One man thinks in terms
of the public, and according to his degree of development he may be a caterer, entertainer, politician,
writer, or teacher. Another thinks in terms of
conquest, and may thus be an explorer, soldier,
pioneer, or reformer. One comes under the lunar
influence or the yellow ray, the other under the
martian influence or red ray. One answers to the
number 2 and to vibrations of that number, the
other to the number 9 and its vibrations. But 2
may develop to the higher expression of the lunar
ray, from yellow to white, the resolvent being, as
universally, 9, *i.e.* strife, energy, effort. Thus:

234——567
9——18
27

———

9

The numbers 2 and 7, 3 and 6, 4 and 5 naturally
balance one another, being each in combination of
value of 9. To complete the series we note that 1
and 8 = 9, leaving 9 as the only digit standing
unpaired.

Thought bears a definite relation to truth inasmuch as it approximates to a true expression of fact
or is removed therefrom. Correct thought is formal
truth, and it follows definite lines towards a conclusion involved in the premises. All consistent
thought, therefore, lends itself to numerical expression because as a formulation of some truth it
responds to the same test—harmony. Our thought
is built up in much the same way as a material
edifice. We select our ground, lay our foundations
on the bed-rock of observed fact, and proceed by the
addition of a variety of materials, which are fitted
in their respective places, until we get a complete
edifice designed and fitted to accommodate its
tenant. Thus we build our thought around a
central idea. It is a geometrical structure and
answers at all points to the law of numbers.

The number 1 represents the straight line,
whether by level or plumb; it is the symbol of
integrity, of rectitude.

2 indicates parallelism, comparison, correlation,
and relativity.

3 denotes mensuration and the bringing together of things in apposition upon the common basis of fact, as positive and negative are united in force, force and matter in existence, man and woman in humanity, wisdom and love in God. The Indian Trimurti, or threefold aspect of the Deity, employs Brahma the Creator, Vishnu the Sustainer, and Shiva the Resolver or Destroyer of the universe. The planets answering to these are Jupiter, Mars, and Saturn, and their corresponding colours are violet, indigo, and red. Violet is the combination of the other two. So life and death are both involved in the process of creation. We cannot add anything to the sum-total of matter in the universe nor to that of force. Neither can we take away from the sum-total of either. But we can convert both. Hence, in the building up of thought, we are continually converting and rearranging materials and energy we have already used. Our various expressions of truth as we see it are merely kaleidoscopic, and the same pieces of coloured glass go into the making of our transformations. The conservation of energy, the indestructibility of matter, and the law of permutations are the controlling factors of all human thought. Thought is only a process of mensuration, and it is grounded in form. For this reason we cannot ultimately escape the anthropomorphic conception of Deity. All thought, to be definite, must have form, and form involves material. Hence, because the property of form is dimension, our thought is compassed by the geometrical laws and answers to number.

Architecture, machinery, construction of any kind, as the embodiment of our thought, fully illustrates the fact that our thought is governed by geometrical laws.

Having arrived at this conclusion, we may next observe that our thought bears a definite relation to our environment. The questions that arise in our minds are in direct response to some stimulus from without. The pressure of circumstance requires a continual adjustment of our thought to our environment. The thought of others is as much a part of our circumstance as is their bodily presence ; we have to make room for it and take it into our consideration. Every man is the centre of his own universe, and no two persons can occupy exactly the same position. Consequently, he cannot hold exactly the same point of view in regard to anything except the central fact of Being. As embodied entities we occupy a position somewhere on the periphery of things and answer to a particular point in the *zodiacus vitæ* or circle of living things. In the circle here shown let A represent the central fact of Being from which, by an extension of itself in any particular plane in all directions, it eventuates in the periphery or circumference of being known as physical life, or the external world. Let B and C represent ultimate points of opposite radii, and D a point at a certain angular distance from both. Connected as they are by their radii with the central fact A, they will all regard it alike. But if we posit a relative fact F, we shall see that B, C, D each take different views of it. and between the viewpoints of B and D, and those of C and D, there is formed an angle of parallax, which from their relative standpoints gives the impression of a mental squint.

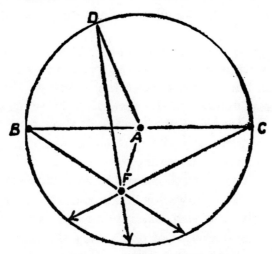

The fact that no two people look at things from exactly the same point of view is the reason why we are all so interesting to one another, and finally so necessary. It is by finding out how the facts of life strike different persons that we are able to get at the truth about it. If we want the true position of an elevated body we have to take the angle of parallax formed by looking at it from two different positions simultaneously and "splitting the difference." This method of splitting the difference is a practical means of getting at the truth about a thing when opinions differ. The difficulty is to know what obliquity is represented by each observer. But if the observers B, D, C identify themselves with the centre at A, then the fact F will appear to all alike, and its true position in the scale of things will be at once apparent by direct perception. This direct perception is only possible to those identified with the Central Fact. All else have only an oblique perception.

In meteorology we take the state of the barometer and the direction of pressure of the wind in a number of detached places throughout the country. From these we can determine the area of depression, and this, with the course of the wind, will show how the weather is travelling. We take the trend of public opinion in exactly the same way, but by different standards. The statistician reduces all his facts to the numbers, and draws his conclusions from those numbers. By the use of numbers it would be possible to make a chart of one's daily thought.

In the East they have a science of numbers which has direct reference to the things of our thought. An illustration of this science will be found in *Kab.*, i. ch. ix.; and another system of numbers by which things lost may be recovered if distinctly thought of. This latter method is based on the belief that a particular thought-form gives rise to and has definite relations with a particular number. Wherefore, if a lost article be thought of and immediately afterwards a number given, this number is a natural sequence of the thought-form, to which it is related by a law of mind. Then by the use of certain pointers or keys involved in the number, the lost article may be found. I am told by some correspondents that they cannot use the formula so as to get correct results. At the International Club for Psychic Research, three successive experiments resulted in as many successful findings. I frequently use the method for friends and associates. In one instance a legal friend had lost some valuable papers containing a precis of a case and a bill of costs wanted for immediate dispatch. In his dilemma he appealed to me, and I at once told him that he would find it on a shelf in his office among some other papers, and suggested including the mantelpiece as a shelf. Having already searched all shelves in the office, he was struck by the last suggestion and at once turned to the mantelpiece, on which stood a folding cupboard ; and on this, among papers of various sorts relating to almost everything except his business, he at once found the paper. Another reader of the *Kabala* wrote me soon after its publication informing me that by its aid he had found a valuable document which covered a considerable sum of money, and which he had long sought for in vain. Obviously, there is a certain spontaneity of mental action required. The process should be as automatic as possible. Some persons are incapable of this automatism; others cannot avoid in, being defective in the faculty of direction of thought.

There remains, however, in the presence of many failures on the part of particular individuals, quite sufficient evidence of the working of a law of mind by which numbers come to have a significance other than that of mere quantity. They are found to have direct relation to the nature of our thought by their correspondence with natural objects in which we are interested and which, as thought-forms stored in the memory, can at any time be evoked and brought forth by their numerical correspondences. That is how things suggest one another in the process known as the association of ideas. Nature would appear to be subject to the same law of numerical sequence, and in these pages I shall be able to show how numbers, or their sound equivalents, follow one another in rotation.

What we know in science as the law of periodicity is but another instance of the rhythmic sequence of vibrations, another name for the Kabalistic doctrine of numerical sequence. In astronomy we have a law of cycles by which the orderly sequence of celestial phenomena can be followed. The Metonic Cycle of 19 years gives us the dates on which the lunations will recur. The Saros of 18 years 10–11 days enables us to trace the sequence of eclipses. The cycle of 649 years gives us the entire range of all eclipses, and after this period they recur in the same order and in the same part of the zodiac. The cyclic law may also be traced in the recurrence of other celestial phenomena, such as the conjunctions of the planets and the recurrence of these in the same part of the zodiac. If Nature observes these cyclic and periodic laws, then assuredly man must reflect them in his constitution, and, through his dependence on physical conditions, in his thought also. These cycles or series of changes in man are proportioned to his average span of years, and whereas Nature has a cycle of

870 years, man has one of 8·7 years. This periodic law appears to be at the root of the old Alfridaries, of which I have given an example in *Kab.*, i. ch. xiii. An ancient Egyptian Alfridary divides the stream of life into two branches called the Sun and Moon, or the Light and Dark Paths. If a child is born during the daytime he is under the influence of the Sun and follows the Sun Path ; but if born at night he follows the Moon Path. By daytime is understood the period from sunrise to sunset, and night is the period from sunset to sunrise. Then they divide the life into periods of five years each, which they set under the planets in their Chaldean order, and from the combined action of the two sets of planetary influence, the Solar and the Lunar, they determine certain climacteric periods in the life of the child then born. The following is the Table of the Sun and Moon Paths, showing the ages at which the planets rule according to the Egyptian scheme.

The years 1, 4, 8, 11, 15, 18, 22, etc., are formative and creative, involving organic changes. The years 5, 7, 12, 14, 19, 21, etc., are chaotic and destructive. The years 8, 13, 20, etc., are increscent and beneficial. It is difficult to say how they applied these set alfridaries to individual cases, but they serve to show that a law of periodic was more than hinted at in their speculations.

[TABLE.

4

Table of Sun and Moon Paths

Sun			*Moon*	
☉	☉	1	☽	☽
	☿	2	♀	
	♀	3	☿	
	☽	4	☉	
	♁	5	♄	
	♃	6	♃	
	♄	7	♂	
☿	☉	8	☽	♀
	☿	9	♀	
	♀	10	☿	
	☽	11	☉	
	♂	12	♄	
	♃	13	♃	
	♄	14	♂	
♀	☉	15	☽	☿
	☿	16	♀	
	♀	17	☿	
	☽	18	☉	
	♂	19	♄	
	♃	20	♃	
	♄	21	♂	
☽	☉	22	☽	☉
	☿	23	♀	
	♀	24	☿	
	etc.		etc.	

The successive periods of 4, 8, 10, 19, 15, 12, and 30 years, following the order of the planetary velocities, are well known in association with the Seven Ages of Man. They are referred to in the comedy *As You Like It*, and take the following form :—

1– 4 years,	Childhood—Variability. ☽
4–12 ,,	Schooling—Knowledge. ☿
12–22 ,,	Courtship—Love. ♀
22–41 ,,	Ambition—Virility. ☉
41–56 ,,	Concentration—Intensity. ♂
56–68 ,,	Fulfilment—Maturity. ♃
68–98 ,,	Decline—Senility. ♄

The recognition of this cyclic law in human development is a plenary acknowledgment of the fact that the phenomena of life answer to numerical sequence, and if we understand that the phenomenal world is the reflex of the numerical, we shall of course require that number is the controlling factor in the development and expression of human thought. Moreover, we cannot begin to study the laws of cosmos, nor those of any science whatsoever, without recourse to numbers as a means of expressing those laws. Therefore whatever we think of the universe or of natural phenomena must finally lend itself to numerical expression. Measure, capacity, density, bulk, gravity, velocity, weight, proportion, are all comprehended in number, the perception of which is the determining factor of mental acumen. We see therefore that mentality is grounded in the perception of quantitative relations and thus in numbers.

CHAPTER IV

NUMBER IN RELATION TO FEELING

WHEN Goethe called a cathedral "frozen music" he was expressing that sense of the relations of sound and form which invests the words of every poet. What Goethe apprehended by the instinct of poesy as rhythmic structure, science has later developed experimentally in such part that we are able to say that certain forms correspond with and are the natural embodiment of sound. The eidophone and phonograph produce definite records of sound, and it has been found that the same forms are constantly reproduced from the same sounds. By this knowledge the science of acoustics was immensely enlarged. The eidophone is a simple apparatus that anybody can construct. It consists of a tin funnel with an extended tube of the same material elbowed so as to form a stem to the funnel like that of a tobacco-pipe. Across the mouth of the funnel a sheet of thin guttapercha is stretched very tightly and tied round to keep it taut and secure. On top of this membrane is placed some podophyllin, lycopodium, or other light powder. A note being sounded down the aperture, the powder will rise into the air by the vibration of the membrane, and will fall back again in a definite geometrical form. The notes of the scale being sounded clear and strong from a cornet, each will yield its corresponding form, and a return to the same note will reproduce the same form. A more elaborate instrument employs an ink-pen turning upon a universal joint attached to a needle which is actuated by the vibrations of a wire connected with a tympanum. This instrument reproduces the most complex and beautiful geometrical forms, resulting from a scroll-work of very fine pen-lines.

If you look at the frost-ferns on a frozen pavement or window-pane, you see there the splash of the wind upon the moist surface of the hard body just at the moment when the frost seized it in its icy grip. The whole of visible Nature is an embodiment of vibrations, and the ancient belief was that the first forms were produced from plastic world-stuff by the Logos or Word, by which all things were created. " And God said : Let there be——, and it was so."

We all learn to interpret these sound-forms as soon as we learn the mother-tongue. We cannot see the atmospheric forms created by speech, but we have a sense-organ that registers them, and we read them off by sensation of hearing—at first singly, then by twos and threes, and lastly by phrases. Sound-forms that appeal to us through the sense of sight have also a meaning, but the science of symbolism is not so fully developed that we can understand this process of signalling by form so well as we do that of signalling by sound. The semaphore and helioscope are less in vogue than the telephone and phonograph, and they are very clumsy in comparison with them. How little we take the meaning of Nature's form-message is seen by the commonplace response to a perfect conspiracy of form and colour. "Pretty place," says one. "Very pretty," says another—and that is an end of impressions. What it *means* is beyond them. The geologist, the naturalist, the botanist, each catch disjointed sentences. The artist may or may not apprehend its meaning, but he catches all of its feeling. And this brings me to a consideration of vibration in relation to feeling as expressed chiefly in sound and colour.

None can listen to one of Mendelssohn's "Songs without Words" and not be impressed by a definite feeling which, by the highest science of expression, the composer conveys to us in his wonderful melodies. You know that he is portraying a definite sequence of emotions, and you feel those emotions in yourself. He made no use of words to define them, nor have you need of words to feel them, but he nevertheless succeeds as fully in conveying his feeling by music without the use of words, as a poet does by words without the use of music. Hence we see that, as regards feeling, which in effect is all there is of life or in it, the language of music and the language of words are of equal value. But there is this in language that does not pertain to music. It is capable of stirring up strife, which no music ever did. The nearest to it I have ever heard was produced by chromatic discords at quick time, and was intended to indicate a rabble.

The natural scale bears a definite relation to cosmical factors, and because the planets correspond with colours and numbers, there is a harmony, through cosmic sequence, between sound, colour, and number. Thus :

Planet, etc.	Note.	Colour.	Number.
Saturn . .	D	Indigo	8
Jupiter. .	B	Violet	3
Mars . .	G	Red	9
Sun . .	C	Orange	1 or 4
Venus . .	A	Blue	6
Mercury .	E	Yellow	5
Moon . .	F	Green	7 or 2

These colours and their planetary correlates differ somewhat from the Table given on p. 60, *Kab.* i., the variants of Saturn, Mercury, and Moon, in terms of our physical perception, being there given in order to include the nine digits. The above Table may, however, be regarded as correct in regard to the primary relations of colour and number.

If we examine these colour relations—remember always that colour is our perception of definite rates of etheric vibration—we shall find some interesting correspondences. Thus :

Saturn is regarded astrologically as the " melan-

choly " planet, its sobering influence when prominent in the horoscope at birth being very marked.
It was rising in conjunction with Mercury and the
Sun at the birth of Dante, "the man who went
down into hell"; and rising also in that of Edgar
A. Poe, "the night owl" of poetry. It held
the highest position in the horoscope of Napoleon,
"the man of destiny." It is generally prominent
in the horoscopes of the philosophers, and it
induces to depth of thought whenever it dominates
the mind. Hence indigo is allied to the melan-
cholic, and its primary significance is steadfastness.
In contra-distinction to these we find orange and
deep yellow, the vital and active colours.

Jupiter, the optimistic planet, indicating expansion, hopefulness, etc., has relation to the colour
violet. It is the colour produced by passing a
white ray through a very thin sheet of silver, and
is related to the auric envelope of the normal
man in the same way as green is to the astral body.
In the Indian cosmogony we find Brahma, the
Creator (from the root *Brih*, to expand), investing
the *Brahmándam*, or egg of the universe, wherein,
by expansion of himself, the universe is created.
Hence we trace a connection between Brahma and
Jupiter (*Deo-pitar* = the Father God), and between
Jupiter and the aura, or egg of individuality. In
esotericism this is the persistent vehicle of the
imperishable and evolving monad. It is cosmically
referred to as *hiranyagarbha* or Golden Egg, and
represented as floating in the waters of space, while
over it is seen *Kálahamsa*, or the Swan of Time. As

by the expansion of the One Self the universe was created, so by the expansion of the individual the fulness of life is attained. Jupiter therefore as *Brihaspati*, or Lord of Expansion, corresponds with violet, the colour of the vital optimist.

When Jupiter is prominent in the horoscope we find that optimism and power of expansion are characteristics of those then born. The planet was rising in the horoscope of King Edward VII., in that of Lord Northcliffe, and others of this temperament. The number 3, corresponding with Jupiter and violet, is seen also to represent " *ovals* and bodies capable of *expansion* and *contraction* " (*Kab.*, i. 59). Violet is essentially the colour of Hope.

Mars, the ruddy planet, is seen to correspond with the flamboyant note G, with the colour red or crimson, and the number 9. The association of Mars with all forms of hurt and strife is well known. From *marna*, to strike, we have *marta*, killing, and such derivatives as to murder, to mar, martial, etc. Among forms we have " all sharp, keen, and pointed things—spears, lances, scalpels, swords, knives, flints, and tongues of flame." The connection between " tongues of flame " and inspiration is familiar through the Pentecostal fire. Nine is the number of regeneration, of spirituality, freedom, self-extension, and pervading. Mars is associated with Vishnu, the energiser of the created universe, from *Vish*, to pervade. Fire, intensity, zeal, ardour, and keenness are all characteristic of the planet Mars so far as its cosmic qualities are represented in human character; thus its associations

with the colour red are therefore so appropriate
as barely to need comment.   All these qualities,
characteristics, colours, and sounds, that are ascribed
to the planets obtain their significance for us by
reason of their appeal to our feeling, through consciousness.   Colour, form, etc., have no qualities
per se.   It is we who invest them with such, and we
do so because of the influence they exert upon our
emotions.   When we listen to music we are conscious of certain emotions stirring in us, and we
attribute to the music all that we experience in
ourselves.   The truth is that there is nothing in the
music itself but the series of rhythmic vibrations of
which it consists, and these are in reality perfectly
noiseless atmospheric motions which attain the
significance of sound only when they enter our consciousness.   What we feel is what the musician felt
when he was composing, and he made use of the
language of music to express his feelings.   If we
would really know how much feeling there is in
language *per se*, and beyond what we impart to it,
try some Choctaw language on the first man you
meet, and, unless he is an American polyglot, he
will probably suggest that you ask a policeman, or
tell you that he feels like that himself sometimes,
and will encourage you to work it all off before
going home.

Venus is the acknowledged representative of
music, art, poetry, and all the finer sentiments of
the human mind.   It is the embodiment of the
rhythmical, the sympathetic—in a word, of *harmony*.
It embraces all the harmonious and rhythmic arts—

dancing, music, poetry, painting,—and all industries
in which the artistic element is the principal factor.
Its colour, blue, is in the nature of an anodyne—
soothing, pacifying, and non-irritant. It is on the
negative side of the spectrum and absorbs the
yellows. Blue as a nerve-rester is well known and
fully employed by chromopathic healers, such as
Babbit, Albertini, and others. In the pathology of
colour, blue is the tone used for allaying irritation
and the effects of nervous corrosion. It answers to
the note A, and by a certain fitness of things this
note is used in orchestration as the pitch-note by
which all instruments are brought into accord.
The celestial vestment of the Madonna is that blue
which represents mercy, loving-kindness, purity,
and grace—in a word, harmony.

Mercury is related to the colour yellow, which is
the most luminiferous of the spectrum. Mercury
corresponds to the intelligence principle of the mind,
the perceptive and rational faculties, and their
appropriate memories. Ptolemy, in his *Tetrabliblos*,
says that the Moon governs the natural or animal
soul and Mercury the human or rational soul, the
epithemia and *phrēn* of the Greek classification.
Light is that which reveals all form and colour, and
Mercury, as indicating luminosity, is thus the
Awakener, the Anubis of the Egyptian theogony,
the wolf-headed god who awakened the Sleeping
Souls and conducted them to the Hall of Judgment.
The Hebrew equivalent is Ish-caleb (man-wolf),
from which the Greeks derived their Æsculapius,
the god of medicine. Knowledge, as represented

by Mercury, is the one cure for that great disease of
mind known as ignorance. Man is agnostic until
the messenger of the gods brings him the torch-
light of revelation ; then he is gnostic, and joins the
followers of Hermes. Yellow unites with blue
(Venus) to form the Nature-colour, green. So
Hermes and Aphrodite, Mercury and Venus, unite
to form the Hermaphrodite, or natural man. So
6 Venus and 5 Mercury unite to form $11 = 2$, the
number of the Moon, which corresponds in our
table to green. When Mercury, the intelligence
principle, is united to its ethereal counterpart, the
result is enlightenment. The Gnostics spoke of
two aspects of the mind, and above the sphere of the
Christos, or Mercury (messenger), they placed the
sphere of Eros. Mercury is represented as bearing
the caduceus, the Hellenised form of the Hebrew
Qedeshi-ash, or Fire of the Holy Ones. The idea
that it is the symbol of Peace is very modern and
incorrect. It represents the interaction of the *Ida*
and *Pingala*, or male-female creative fires, united in
the *Shushumna*, and the rod is the Brahmadandam,
or spinal column, represented by the bamboo stick
of the yogi, with its notches or nodes corresponding
with the nervous ganglia of the spinal process. It
stands for the Hermetic Art or Secret Knowledge.
Mercury in this capacity of staff-bearer is akin to
Prometheus, who brought the fire of the gods
down in a fennel-stalk for the use of mankind. As
interpreter of the gods, Mercury represents the
faculty of translation By knowledge of universal
symbolism we are enabled to translate form into

words, colour into sound, and both into number. By the alchemy of the mind, represented by Hermetic Art, we transmute feeling into thought and thought into feeling. It is through the intelligence principle, therefore, that number as represented by Mercury is capable of a direct correspondence with feeling. The number of Mercury is 5, and it is the Nature-number which stands for embodied humanity. In the *Book of Lo* the ancient Chinese embodied the symbolism of Nature in the form of a " Square of Three " (*Kab.*, i. p. 41), where 5, the symbol of man the Cogniser, is centred, contributing to the 10 of a perfected environment the value of cognition, which converts the totality of phenomena (10) into the totality of noumena (15), and thus gives to Nature the functions of divinity, the stature of the God-man being represented by the number 15.

The *Moon* is related to two numbers, 7 being the positive aspect and 2 the negative. As 7 it is the full Moon acting in opposition to the Sun, when we get the combination $1 + 7 = 8$ sinister ; and at the New Moon the value 2 in combination with the Sun, number $1 = 3$, which is a fortunate number, being increscent, whereas 8 is decrescent, for 3 is the number of Jupiter and denotes expansion, and 8 is that of Saturn and denotes contraction. In conjunction with the Sun the Moon is negative, or female ; while in opposition it is positive, or male. Here, the Romans, following the more ancient custom of the Sabeans and Hebrews, instituted a festival to Juno-Lucina, at which the people changed

garments for those of the opposite sex.   So, while
the Moon's body was called *Lebenah* by the Hebrews,
the soul of it was *Gebur*—one being " the fair," and
the other " the strong."

The number of the Moon being 2, it denotes
relativity, vacillation, change ; but as 7 it denotes
fulness, stability (*Kab.*, i. 8).   In the Hebraic
system the numbers followed the days of the week,
namely :

Sunday	☉	1–8
Monday	☽	2–9
Tuesday	♂	3
Wednesday	☿	4
Thursday	♃	5
Friday	♀	6
Saturday	♄	7

And this system is interpreted in *Kab.*, i. ch. i.
Here it is seen that the numbers 1 and 8, Life and
Death, are vested in the Sun's influence ; while 2 and
9, denoting change and strength, are ascribed to the
Moon The *Geburim* (Geber = strength) were a
race of spiritual warriors, and the angel Gabriel is
always represented as invested with great power.
He it is who is said to have led Israel through its
victorious campaign on the way to Palestine.   The
Kabalists, however, regard the angel as the Angel
of Grace, a type of the Higher Ego, or Christ-
principle in man, and in their interpretation Egypt
is the physical body (Capricorn = Saturn), the
House of Bondage and darkness ; the wilderness is
the period of probation in the world ; the Hivites,

Perizzites, Gergashites, Jebuzites, and Amalekites
are the various passions and evil principles that
" he who would prevail " (Israel) has to overcome
before he can pass through the baptism of Jordan
(yar-din), or River of Spiritual Knowledge, and enter
the Promised Land of his spiritual heritage.   Therefore, in the Yetzirah, or Transformations, they trace
man through the cadence of his incarnations from
the Sun (the spiritual state) to Saturn (the state of
spiritual darkness), and then back again from
Saturn to the Sun.

The Moon has always been identified with the
Earth, and in symbolical systems, which have
regard to the point of view of embodied man, the
Moon is set between the planets Venus and
Mars.   Its colour, green, is that resulting from the
admixture of blue and yellow, the colours of Venus
and Mercury, and, as we have seen, the numbers
of these planets, 6 and $5 = 11 = 2$, the number of the
Moon (negative).   Now, green is the colour of the
Earth's livery, and is the Nature-colour, having its
place in the midst of the spectrum between the
blues and yellows.

Now, if we regard the blues as denoting Thought
and the yellows as denoting Feeling, we get in green
a combination of the two as the colour-symbol of
the natural man.   In ancient belief the souls of men
came to earth through the Moon sphere.   Occultists
do not regard this as referring to the Moon as a body,
but to that circumferential sphere of the astral
plane which, according to the principles of gravitation, would lie outside and around the earth as far

as the orbit of the Moon. The confusion of the names Selene (the Moon) and Selinon (parsley) sufficiently explain why, according to the tradition of dames, children are born in the parsley-bed, why preparations of parsley are used as emmenagogues, and perhaps also why old herbalists call it the "lunatic herb" and place it under the dominion of the Moon.

Here I may bring out the relations of the planetary colours according to this scheme of correspondences in a diagrammatic form.

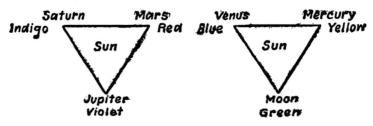

If we take a leaf out of the Hindu theogony we shall find this scheme exactly repeated, with the exception that Saturn and Jupiter change places so as to be brought into numerical order. Thus Saturn, Jupiter, and Mars represent the Trimurti or male trinity of deific aspects—Shiva, Brahma, and Vishnu; but they are always put in this order, Brahma, Vishnu, Shiva, *i.e.* Jupiter, Mars, Saturn; the Creator, Energiser or Preserver, and Regenerator or Destroyer.

"It maketh and unmaketh, mending all;
   What it hath wrought is better than had been;
 Slow grows the splendid pattern that it weaves
   Its subtle hands between!"

Then the S'aktis or female counterparts of the Prajapatis or Lords are set in apposition thus:

♃ Brahma—Saraswati ☿
♂ Vishnu—Lakshmi ♀
♄ Shiva—Parvati ☽

These are their cosmic gods and goddesses, but the manifestation of the Supreme Deity is Krishna, the Sun-born.

Hence it appears there are various aspects of one and the same truth, the fact being that from whatever point of view we regard Nature we shall find her full of correspondences and symbols, and at all times answering to a numerical law, because it is we who impose those correspondences and make use of those symbols, and because also they answer to a law of mind which is vested in numerical ratios, or rather in our perception of quantitive relations. Without man as cogniser Nature would hold no such significance. It is not a self-conscious aggregate. Consciousness seems to begin when Life comes into relations with matter at a certain stage of its development, and self-consciousness when Mind takes possession of the vitalised organisms. Consciousness, therefore, appears to result from the strain set up between energy and matter through resistance, and self-consciousness from the relations of soul to environment, or mind-force in association with organic matter. The first results in sensation, the last in Feeling. The position that what we call inanimate matter shows sensation-consciousness by its response to stimulus has already been argued

5

(*Cosmic Symbolism*), and there is no need to do more than affirm it in this place. As sensation is the beginning of consciousness, so Feeling is the end of self-consciousness. The evolution of man is through his sensorium, and finally he must become a perfected sensory creature capable of the highest expressions of Feeling. The highest form of feeling is Sympathy—another name for syntonic vibration. Number, as represented by vibration, lies at the root of all being, and invests colour, form, sound with all the significance they have for us. We may apprehend them intellectually, but they do not become part of us until we feel them.

The scheme here presented of Colours and Numbers in relation to Thought and Feeling may be summarised thus :

Jupiter—Violet,	3—Hope, optimism, expansion.	
Saturn—Indigo,	8—Contemplation, philosophy.	
Venus—Blue,	6—Purity, spirituality, peace.	
Moon—Green,	2—Sensation, variability.	
Mercury—Yellow,	5—Mind, intellection, perception.	
Sun—Orange,	4—Vitality, force.	
Mars—Red,	9—Zeal, energy, intensity.	

We may observe that Orange, the Sun colour, becomes red, Mars, when vitality becomes concentrated. Then we get zeal, intensity, and ardour as the effects of the vital powers being brought to a focus and directed along specific channels towards the accomplishment of some particular object. It is in accord with the Doctrine of Correspondences that we should regard Number as related to Thought

and Colour to Feeling. That one corresponds with
and gives rise to the other is evident by natural
science and psychology. Consequently we find
Number more immediately connected with Science,
and Colour with Art, the one being capable of intellectual demonstration, the other of artistic
expression. Therefore, Science (Mercury) is considered as masculine and exterior, while Art
(Venus) is regarded as feminine and interior. The
consideration that the more interior is the more
spiritual leads to the higher appreciation of Art as
the expression of Feeling. From the point of view
of evolution, the artist is therefore in advance of
the man of science, and in all systems of symbolism
Venus is placed above Mercury, and it is interesting
to note that among the planetary orbits Mercury
shows the greatest divergence from the circular, *i.e.*
its eccentricity is greatest, while Venus shows the
least, its orbit being all but a perfect circle. In
days to come, when Venus makes an orbit that is
perfectly symmetrical, the world will get a perfect
expression of Feeling as developed in Art. The
post-impressionist of modern evolution is a decadent
scion of Venus. He only portrays Nature as reflected in a cracked mirror. He has no constant
plane of perception and no fixed view-point. Consequently he depicts a man's left optic as in the
middle of his forehead, his right ear where his nose
should be, and the lapels of his coat on the back of
his neck. In an age of buffoonery the effort to be
original must needs lead to some strange effects ;
but Feeling should be the *lingua sancta* of the true

exponent of Art, and reversion to standards of Beauty in colour and form—in a word, naturalness —will be his only legitimate means of progress.

Bringing our researches regarding Colour and Number into line with what has been observed regarding Sound, we find the correspondence of primaries to result as here shown :

Planet	.	☉	♄	☿	☽	♂	♀	♃
Note	.	C	D	E	F	G	A	B
Number	.	4–1	8	5	7–2	9	6	3
Colour	.	Orange	Indigo	Yellow	Green	Red	Blue	Violet

The notes C, E, G form a common chord. Their corresponding numbers are 4, 5, 9, so that $4+5$ coalesce in 9 ; also D, F, A form a chord, and their numbers are 8, 7, 6 ; thus bringing $8+7=15=6$ into harmony with 6. I cannot say where the observation may lead to, but I have noted it as suggestive ; and I may add that Saturn 8 and Moon 7 are astrologically in terms with Venus 6, inasmuch as the two signs Libra and Taurus are ruled by Venus, and are the exaltation signs of Saturn and the Moon respectively.

CHAPTER V

NUMBERS AND INDIVIDUALS

It would be possible to argue a connection between Numbers and Volition in the same way as we have seen it to exist in relation to Thought and Feeling; but as all will is expressed in thought and feeling which ultimates as speech and action, or word and deed, it will be convenient and probably far more interesting if we trace this association of Will and Number in the ultimate fact of birth, showing the expression and limitations of the will by reference to the date of birth and other data incidental to particular cases.

It will be well, however, if we have a clear idea of the Correspondence in the Scale of Manifestation through which we argue from Divine principles to human activity, and thus from unity into diversity. Assuming the Sun, as centre of the system, as expressing the Logos, we have the two conditions of Light and Heat corresponding with Divine Wisdom and Love, the two being united in the single body of the Sun, or the Divine Substance. Things that correspond are not identical, but the material is dependent on the spiritual as body upon soul, and

the inferior or dependent state of existence is the
expression of the superior. The words inferior and
superior may be regarded as equivalent to exterior
and interior in this connection. Light reveals
forms, heat gives them life. In gross darkness
nothing exists as form, and in a state of ignorance
there is no true definition of things. Heat animates
and fills all forms of life with energy. At the poles,
where there is less heat than at other parts of the
earth, there is less animation. Rays of light may be
artificially slowed down and converted into heat
rays. By offering resistance to an electric current
one may obtain light. Thought and Feeling are
thus convertible. What lies at the back of Light
and Heat, or Thought and Feeling, is Energy or
Life, and this is the source of Volition. From these
and other considerations we may derive the Scale of
Correspondences as follows :—

Life

Wisdom—Love

Volition

Truth—Charity

Desire

Knowledge—Affection

Thought—Feeling

Speech—Action

Character.

Here we see Life as Volition and Desire ultimating
as Character or Conduct, the expressions of human
life in speech and action. The Scale of Correspondences shows the related pairs of principles on the

Divine, spiritual, and human planes. In this scheme
of thought every life is a partial expression of the
One Life, and every phase of human character and
destiny is the reflex, under limitation, of the One
Intelligence and Will. The idea is laid hold of by
Armand Silvestre:

"Thou art Cause Supreme of Life,
  The hidden Good in every ill—
Which even they who live in strife
  Do serve with an unconscious will,—
Thou art the salve of hearts that bleed,
  The grave of every ruined creed!"

We may therefore safely explore the diversities
of character and destiny from the point of view that
all is subservient to the main purpose of creation,
and a reflection—perhaps also a refraction—of the
divine will as expressed in number and regulated
by cosmic laws.

I have already shown (*Kab.*, i. ch. iv.) that man
answers to a certain numerical plan known as the
"Square of Three." He is embodied cosmos, and,
being compounded of cosmic elements, he responds
to the planets of the solar system, and to the numbers,
colours, sounds, and forms associated with them.

What may be the law of the supramundane it is
not our purpose to inquire. Man as we know him
is such as he is by reason of embodiment. The
fact of birth is the result of cosmic law acting
through the individual. The evolution of an entity
is wrapped up in the circumstance of birth, the time
and conditions being dependent on inherent character and faculty. The making of gods out of men

is a long process, and we have no reason to suppose
that it is compassed in one life or even one hundred
lives.   But, in order to illustrate our insistent law
of numerical ratios, it will be necessary to make use
of a number of striking instances, restricting ourselves to the one life that is presently patent to us.

It has already been shown that the Moon represents the element of variability, and that its numbers
are 2 and 7.   It is proposed to show that the sign
occupied by the Moon at the birth of a person is
that which, by its planetary and numerical affinity,
controls or determines the particular characteristic
that is dominant in that person.

Granted for the moment that the premiss of
astrology is valid, and that the disposition of the
cosmic factors at the moment of birth is the key to
character and fortunes, then it will follow that,
inasmuch as the Moon's apparent motion in the
zodiac is the greatest, and that whereas the Sun
remains in the same sign for a month, and other of
the celestial bodies for many months together,
while the Moon passes from one sign to the next in
the space of only sixty hours, it must be of chief
importance in the estimate of individual faculty,
character, and even destiny.   Such, indeed, we find
it, although it is not that which finally determines
the line of individual evolution.

In order to examine these cases in the light of the
values already ascribed to the numbers 1 to 9, we
shall have to give a value to each of the signs in
terms of the planet which has affinity with each.
Thus :

Aries and Scorpio signs, of Mars, answer to number 9
Taurus and Libra,   „   Venus   „   6
Gemini and Virgo,   „   Mercury   „   5
Cancer, ruled by the Moon,   „   2 and 7
Leo ruled by the Sun,   „   1 and 4
Sagittarius and Pisces, ruled by Jupiter,   „   3
Capricornus and Aquarius, ruled by Saturn   „   8

Applying these numbers to the position of the
Moon at the birth of several notable persons, it will
be seen that there is sufficient ground for establish-
ing an argument in favour of numerical values as
determined by planetary positions. Vibrations, of
course, lie at the back of the whole scheme. They
are Nature's expression of number, as revealed by
the various modes and rates of motion in the same
etheric medium, giving rise to as many different
natural phenomena, as electricity, light, heat, etc.
Moreover, there is nothing unreasonable in the view
that the Moon may exert a different action on us
from various parts of its orbit. Our zodiacal
divisions may be a convenient method of registering
and classifying these differences.

Take, then, the following examples from among
many at our disposal :

Napoleon I., born 15th August 1769. Moon in
Capricornus, number 8, ruled by Saturn. Saturn
in Cancer, number 7. Here we have the combination of a strong egotism, denoted by the
number 7, and fatality denoted by the number 8.
The disturbance of the equilibrium or *status quo*
in the concert of nations is well defined by the

position of the Moon in the sign of Saturn, answering to the sinister influence of the number 8. This is the number of dissolution, of cyclic evolution, reaction, revolution, fracture, disintegration, decomposition, anarchism, lesion, separation, and divorce.

The Moon being in the sign of Saturn, and Saturn in the sign of the Moon, there was a particular strengthening of the fatal egotism which determined the destinies of the great general.

King Henry of Navarre. According to Morinus the Moon was in Aries, ruled by Mars, number 9. Born 13th December (O.S.) 1553.   Here we have the scion of Mars, answering to the high vibration of liberty and conquest indicated by the number 9. But Mars, being in the sign of Saturn—namely, Capricornus—answering to the number 8, there was a sinister resolution to his career, which ended in his murder at the hands of Ravaillac.

Queen Alexandra, born 1st December 1844. Moon in Leo, ruled by the Sun, number 1.   Dignity, honour, prestige, success, distinction, rulership. Sun in Sagittarius, ruled by Jupiter, number 3. Generosity, expansiveness, increase, benevolence. The combination of Sun, Moon, and Jupiter is very fortunate.

" Carmen Sylva," Queen of Roumania.   Moon in Aries, ruled by Mars, number 9.   Penetration, incisiveness, courage, fortitude, determination, zeal.   Mars in Pisces, ruled by Jupiter, number 3. Generosity, increase, and good works.   Impulsiveness.

Charles I. of England. Moon in Libra, ruled by Venus, number 6. Venus in Sagittarius, ruled by Jupiter, number 3. This combination indicates a strong artistic sense, gentleness, suavity, love of peace and harmony, fondness for the play, music, dancing, etc. A sociable nature with keen sense of justice and a benevolent disposition.

Joan of Arc, born 6th January 1412. Moon in Libra, ruled by Venus, number 6. Gentleness, suavity, peace, harmony, and love of the beautiful. Venus in Capricorn, ruled by Saturn 8. Disappointment, loss, captivity. A more positive element is found in the horoscope by the conjunction of Moon and Jupiter, and the mental peculiarity is derived from the opposition of Mercury to Neptune.

Annie Besant, born 1st October 1847. Moon in Cancer, number 2. Change, variability, travelling, alternation, publicity. The more positive aspect of the Moon is related to the number 7, and denotes attainment, fulness, completion, satisfaction, equilibrium.

Kaiser Wilhelm II. Moon in Scorpio, ruled by Mars, number 9. Zeal, energy, courage, decision, strength, and endurance. Mars in Pisces, ruled by Jupiter, number 3. Generosity, magnanimity, increase, and good works. Impulsiveness.

Rudyard Kipling. Moon in Gemini, ruled by Mercury, number 5. Intellection, reason, logic, travelling. Mercury in Sagittarius, ruled by Jupiter, number 3. Expansiveness, generosity, increase, success. The horoscopical conjunction of Mercury and Venus shows clearly the poetic bias of the intellect, ruled by Mercury.

Lord Northcliffe. Moon in Aries, ruled by Mars, number 9. Courage, persistence, keenness, penetration, attack. Mars in Virgo, ruled by Mercury, number 5. Alertness, intellection, commerce, astuteness.

Now, if we take these few cases, which might have been multiplied indefinitely, and find the numerical equivalent of the Moon and planetary combination, we shall have the key to the character.

Napoleon I. 2 Moon, 8 Saturn. Sum 10 or 1. Empire, rulership, egotism.

Henry of Navarre. Moon, Mars, Saturn $= 298$ $= 19 = 1$. Rulership, empire, egotism.

Queen Alexandra. Moon, Sun, Jupiter $= 213 = 6$. Gentleness, refinement, harmony, charity.

"Carmen Sylva." Moon, Mars, Jupiter $= 293 = 5$. Intellection, intelligence, alertness.

Charles I. Moon, Venus, Jupiter $= 263 = 2$. Vacillation, variability.

Joan of Arc. Moon, Venus, Saturn $= 268 = 16 = 7$. Attainment, completion, perfection, publicity.

Annie Besant. Moon (in its own sign) $= 2$. Variability, popularity.

Kaiser Wilhelm II. Moon, Mars, Jupiter $= 793 = 19 = 1$. Conquest, empire, egotism.

Rudyard Kipling. Moon, Mercury, Jupiter $= 253 = 10 = 1$. Conquest, dominion, rulership. In the case of a commoner it denotes success, distinction, and authority.

Lord Northcliffe. Moon, Mars, Mercury = 295
= 7. Perfection, completion, attainment, publicity.

It will be observed that we take the Moon as the
basis of the calculation in each case and apply to it
the number of the planet in whose sign it is, ex-
cepting when it is in its own sign, when it is taken
by itself alone, and to these we add the planetary
value for the sign in which the Moon-ruler is found.

Most frequently it will be found that people who
have prominent parts to play in the world have the
Moon-rulers in prominent positions at the time of
birth, so that they come under that ray or vibration
which at the time is the most powerful. Thus
Napoleon, whose Moon-ruler was Saturn, had
Saturn in the mid-heaven of his horoscope. The
present Emperor of Germany, whose Moon-ruler is
Mars, has Mars in the mid-heaven. But this is not
always the case, and it may well be that there are
other combinations of planetary influence producing
vibrations in the constitution to which the singular
prominence of an individual may be attributed.
It is a patent fact, however, that those planets
which hold the four angles of a horoscope—namely,
the Mid-heaven, Ascendant, Descendant, and Nadir
—have always a most marked effect in the character
and destiny of individuals.

Thus in Napoleon's horoscope Saturn was in the
mid-heaven and the Moon in the lower angle. In
King Edward's horoscope (see *Prognostic Astronomy*)
Jupiter was in the eastern angle or Ascendant.
The same was the case with Lord Northcliffe
(*Answers*). Cecil Rhodes had Sun, Moon, and

Venus in the descending angle. Annie Besant had
Uranus rising in the eastern angle, the Moon in the
north angle, Sun, Venus, and Mercury in the west
angle. The German Emperor has Mars in the
mid-heaven. Mr Tom Mann, the socialist, has Sun
and Mercury in the east angle, Mars in the west,
and Venus exceedingly weak. Mr Gladstone (Prime
Minister) had Uranus in the south angle and Sun
and Mercury in the east.

It may be said, in fact, that the more the planets
in a horoscope are angular the more is the subject
of that horoscope impressed with the peculiarities
and potencies of such planets, making in effect a
personality strong enough to force itself into public
notice whether in good or evil. Thus, while it
gives an apparent independence of character,
because of marked individuality, it also brings them
under greater compulsion, and thus in a sense into
greater servitude. For those who attain to positions of great eminence hold them only by continual
effort, untiring watchfulness, and constant anxiety.
The "cynosure for wandering eyes," they must
play their elected part without recess, or sink into
oblivion. Those, on the other hand, in whose
horoscopes the planets are in succeedent positions
owe their measure of success not so much to prominence before the world or to the compulsion of
circumstances, but rather to steadfast endurance
and application, being by nature plodders rather
than pioneers. But when the majority of the
planets are cadent there is seen to be a degree of
indifference to the common ambitions of life and a

peculiar inconsequence of temperament, even in those whose faculties are conspicuous.

Therefore, when we speak of a person answering to the number 9, we do not mean that he is disposed to the more forceful methods of the average Martian, but that he is capable of great intensity of purpose, much zeal, independence of spirit, and freedom of opinion. Then, again, there is the abnormal aspect of this particular red ray of the " nine " vibration. In such case it produces the maniac, the firebrand, the anarchist, and the homicide—the man who " sees red." In a last analysis it will probably be found that Mars and the number 9, the colour red, and all their natural correspondences, signify merely *intensity*. It is as if the vital principle answering to Orange (the Sun) had been brought to a focus, and that from this concentration of the vital principle a species of fever had been induced. All men attain to this fervour of feeling and intensity of purpose and action in their supreme moments; while to genius, and its near neighbour insanity, it is more or less habitual and constant.

Similarly, the man who answers to the vibrations of the planet Jupiter, the violet ray, and the number 3. He may be generous, magnanimous, benevolent, and sympathetic; but also he may be nothing more than a bombast, abounding in excesses and extravagance, jovial, but self-indulgent, and as much indisposed to do harm as good because both entail too much effort and trouble. In either case the expression of the number 3 is *expansion*. In the one case it acts normally by sympathy and altruism, in the other by apathy and egotism. Occasionally we find that a man has nothing more to show for his Jupiterian increscence than an abnormal expansion below the belt. He represents merely the physical side of the number 3. In the two opposite expressions of this type cited above we have the distinction between the blue-violet and the red-violet rays, the limits of this particular order of vibration.

In the Venusian 6 also we have two distinct types, one of which is remarkable for its refinement and culture and the other for its licence and frivolity. Yet the love of harmony is common to both. The number 5 also has a variety of expressions, inasmuch as it primarily answers to intellection ; but it divides easily into a higher and lower aspect of mind, represented by science on the one hand and commerce on the other. The co-operation of these two aspects of mental activity in modern times is a healthy feature tending to intellectual integrity. It is now rightly felt that knowledge is desirable in proportion to its practical utility.

The great range of Mercury's signification, its correspondence with the principle of Mind, and consequently with the varieties of language needed for the expression of mental phases, led to Mercury being regarded as the interpreter or linguist of the gods. Its versatility is well known to astrologers.

Saturn also has two aspects, and its number 8 may signify conservatism or privation That sequestration of the mind peculiar to all philosophers, which enables them to take a detached view of mental and physical phenomena, and so to

formulate the laws of mind and of matter, is one
aspect of the indigo ray and the significance of the
number 8, which probably may be accounted its
highest faculty.   The lower aspect is that which
abides in the dark and cold alleys of a cheerless
misanthropy, finding occasion in the byways of life
to snatch some small advantage from the forget-
fulness or need of another, a sordid miserable type
that finds comfort in privation in order to save
expense.   Between this miserable parasite of the
Earth and the sublime philosopher whose seat is
upon the summit of intellect and whose fearless eye
looks into the very heart of the Sun, there would
appear to be an immeasurable gulf.   Yet it is
bridged by the one word—loneliness.

This isolation, conservatism, insularity, is directly
opposed to the publicity and democratic publicity
of the negative lunar character, responding to the
number 2.

Saturn 8, rules Capricorn ; and the Moon 2, rules
Cancer, the opposite sign.

Similarly we have the dark blue of Saturn
opposed to the yellow of the Moon.

Mars and its corresponding number 9 are allied to
force and strife, while Venus and its number 6 to
persuasion and peace.   Consequently, we find Mars
associated with the signs Aries and Scorpio, opposite
to those of Venus, which are Libra and Taurus.

Thus, while it is extremely easy to " place " an
individual by reason of his dominant characteristic,
whether the intensity of Mars, the pacivity of Venus,
the mutability of the Moon, or the isolation of

6

Saturn, etc., it is by no means so easy to determine the particular grade to which that individual belongs. For, as we have seen, there are extreme poles of any particular ray, colour, or planetary vibration, and between them there are many grades of expression. It would appear that each ray, colour, note, and planet contains a submerged octave in itself, or rather a septenate, so that there may be seven violet sub-rays, or perhaps one pure violet ray with its six sub-rays, making a septenate ; and similarly with the other colours.

Arranged under their planetary symbols they would therefore fall into the following order, number 1 of each series expressing the true characteristic of the particular note, colour, number, or vibration, and number 7 the extreme or abnormal aspect of the dominant characteristic, the intermediate numbers 2 to 6 indicating the variants.

Planetary Variants

Pl.	♄	♃	♂	☉	♀	☿	☽
Col.	Indigo	Violet	Red	Orange	Blue	Yellow	Green
No.	8	3	9	1–4	6	5	7–2
1	♄	♃	♂	☉	♀	☿	☽
2	♃	♀	♄	☽	☽	♂	☿
3	♂	♄	☿	♂	♃	☽	♀
4	☉	☉	☉	☿	☉	☉	☉
5	♀	☽	♃	♃	☿	♄	♂
6	☿	♂	☽	♀	♄	♀	♃
7	☽	☿	♀	♄	♂	♃	♄

It will be observed that the several columns maintain the polarity already referred to, and that this is again repeated along the several lines,— Saturn being polarised by the Moon, Mars by Venus, Jupiter by Mercury; while the central column under the symbol ☉, indicating the vital principle, finds its modifications through the Moon, Mars, etc., and falls into extinction in its negative pole under the

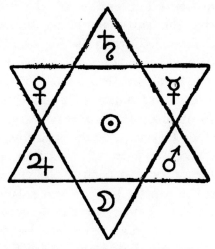

influence of Saturn.   This is conveyed by the astrological paradigm of the Seal of Solomon, which we have elsewhere considered in other relations, wherein these polarities are maintained by the interlacing of the two triangles, representing the spiritual and material, the nominal and phenomenal worlds, in which the positive trigon of Saturn-Jupiter-Mars employs the major planets, and denotes the active male principle; and the negative trigon of Venus-Mercury-Moon, embracing the minor planets, denotes the passive female principle.

From this it would appear that the individual note is that produced by the admixture of a dominant and sub-dominant vibration, as, for example, the Moon being in Taurus, ruled by Venus, answers to that planet and the number 6, colour blue. But Venus being in Pisces, ruled by Jupiter, number 3, we get a composite expression of the Venusian character, under the sub-division of Jupiter, this being found in the third grade of the Venus line of expression. In the Table the vital principle ⊙ 4 is the fulcrum of manifestation, the positive and negative variants being balanced upon this centre line ; and it is of interest to observe that in this scheme the planet Mercury, which was found to be the numerical counterpart of the Sun (*Cosmic Symbolism*), is here seen to occupy the corresponding position in the fourth line of the solar gamut of expression. The Table, which I have called " Planetary Variants," may therefore be regarded also as one expressing Planetary Polarities. The mass of mankind are now in that stage or grade of expression, under these several rays, which is indicated by line 3 of the Table, having emerged from the lower or more animal stage of evolution and attained to the fifth or human stage. Thus one born under Saturn would be manifesting through the sub-ray of Mars ; under Jupiter, through the sub-ray of Saturn ; under Mars, through Mercury ; under the Sun, through Mars ; under Venus, through Jupiter ; under Mercury, through the Moon ; under the Moon, through Venus.

Thus the destructive element of Saturn is expressed in warlike or martial forms ; the theological Jupiter finds philosophical expression ; the zealous Mars gains intellectual and commercial expression ; the vitality of the Solar Man gains forceful or muscular expression in physical culture ; the Venusian art applies to the ecclesiastical ; the principle of intellection has expression in versatility of thought, while commerce is wholly dependent on publication and advertisement; and lastly, the lunar ray of publicity is expressed in the development of artistic effects, and principally applied to pleasure, ease, comfort, and luxury. The net result of all these manifestations of individual character may be called " the Spirit of the Age," the Demagorgon of our sublunary sphere. Of course it will be understood that these ascriptions of the character-notes, colours, numbers, etc., are applicable only to the denizens of our own sphere. On other planets the humanities, being in a more or less advanced stage of evolution, will respond to different gamuts and will be collectively in various stages of those gamuts. The cosmogonic relations of the Martians or the Jovians will place them in subjection to an entirely different astrology, and the various cosmic factors would have to be interpreted in terms of the Martian in the one case, and of the Jovian in the other. If these ascriptions were universal we should argue that the Earth sees these correspondences through a medium of green, or within the vibrations of the

green ray, and thus at once partition our humanity
into the yellow-green (2) and the blue-green (7),
representing the naturals and the intellectuals ;
and all the universe would be in terms of this order
of perception. But there is not the slightest
ground for thinking that these are absolute cosmic
correspondences. On the contrary, it is extremely
probable that the Martian red bears the same relations to the constitution, physical and mental, of
the Martian man, as does the terrestrial green to
ourselves. Unless, therefore, we are prepared to be
extremely complex, we must restrict our study of
character and destiny to their expressions as they
are known to us in our earth-humanity alone, and
leave the wider field to those in whom the self-
extensive faculty is fully developed. It may be of
interest, however, to compare the statements of
that great seer Emanuel Swedenborg concerning
the inhabitants of other planets of the solar system
with the characteristics connoted with them in this
scheme, in which colour, sound, and number are
seen to bear certain well-defined relations to
individuals born under the influence of those
planets. See therefore *Earths of the Universe*, by
Emanuel Swedenborg, in publication by the
Swedenborg Society.

CHAPTER VI

CO-ORDINATION OF VALUES

WE have seen that the expression of Character as
Will has a certain relation to quantitive values.
Will is the human expression of cosmic energy, the
various physical and chemical forces known to us,
and also dynamic force. It therefore has its
numerical relations, because all these cosmic,
chemic, and dynamic forms of energy, another name
for Life, have their mensuration.

If we take the numerical series as comprehended
in the numbers 0 to 9, we shall find that, by continual addition of the odd and even, positive and
negative, male and female numbers, we eventually
derive a further series in which the same values are
present, but in a varied order. In each new series the
value of nine is absent, as shown in the following form:

```
0 1 2 3 4 5 6 7 8 9
 1 3 5 7 9 2 4 6 8
  4 8 3 7 2 6 1 5
   3 2 1 9 8 7 6
    5 3 1 8 6 4
     8 4 9 5 1
      3 4 5 6
       7 9 2
        7 2
         9
```

In the first addition of the digits by pairs we get
the series 1 3 5 7 9, including all the odd numbers,
followed by 2 4 6 8, all the even numbers.   In the
next row the first and last numbers, 4 and 5, pair to
nine, and so of the rest, 3 and 6, 5 and 4, etc. ; but
the number 9 is absent from the series.   It appears
again in the fourth row, but the numbers 4 and 5
are absent.   In the fifth row 9 disappears, but the
equivalent value is lacking in the figures 2 and 7.
In the sixth row 2 3 6 7, making two nines, are
absent.   In the seventh row 1 2 7 8 9, making three
nines, are absent.   In the eighth row 1 3 4 5 6 8,
making three nines, are absent.   In the ninth row
1 3 4 5 6 8 9, making four nines, are absent.   In the
end we have a return to the unit value of nine.
Hence we see that the possible variants of the
complete gamut of expression are ten in number,
and that they finally resolve themselves into the
number nine, which is the symbolical expression of
the Adamic race, the 12×12 or 144, indicated by the
values $ADM = 144$, according to the Hebraic Kabala.

By pairing the first two rows we have 5 nines,
the next two rows yield 4 nines, the next two yield
3 nines, the next two rows give 2 nines, and last two
yield 1 nine.   Hence, from the ten rows we obtain
10, 8, 6, 4, 1, or 29 pairs, falling into the single unit
value of nine.   In this process it will be observed
that the final resolution is *via* the two lunar numbers
7 and 2, one positive, the other negative, and both
answering to the characteristic of variability.   They
are Moon numbers, representing the blue-green and
the yellow-green of the spectrum, and therefore

representing the two aspects of the soul in its
natural or vital development and its spiritual or
mental development.

In this scheme, therefore, we see that the whole
gamut of human expression, so far as it can be
represented by unit values, is included in the
numbers 1–9, and that through successive pairings
or polarisations, we arrive finally through the
element of variability at the single expression of
Humanity = 9. (*Kab.*, i. ch. xv.)

From this scheme also we extract the polarisations
of each numerical type. For observe that whatever line we may take we shall find that the first
and last, second and last but one, etc., in each line,
adds to nine, and is itself an expression of the
Planetary Values which have been determined by
experience to attach to them, and which will be
found fully explained and tested in my book on
Cosmic Symbolism.

In this system the Sun (positive) = 1

Saturn   .   .   8
$$\overline{9}$$

Jupiter answers to the number .   3
Venus to the number   .   .   6
$$\overline{9}$$

Mercury answers to the number .   5
The Sun (negative) to   .   .   4
$$\overline{9}$$

Mars, the tonic of our scale   = 9
Moon, the variable factor, 7 positive
and 2 negative   = 9

These constitute the natural pairs, and, if we regard Mars = 9 as the index of the Man or Microcosm, " made in the image and likeness of Elohim," then 7–2, the numbers of the Moon, will indicate that element of variability which makes for perfection. From this we can derive Bruno's saying: " Infinite variability is the eternal juvenescence of God."

If we take the positive values—1, 3, 5, 7, 9—we find that they correspond with Sun, Jupiter, Mercury, Moon, and Mars, all positive; while the negative values—2, 4, 6, 8—answer to Moon, Sun, Venus, and Saturn in their negative aspects. Pairing these we get from either series the value of 10, leaving 5 unpaired. Hence Ten has been regarded as the Perfect Number, while Five is the number of discrimination, discernment, intellection. It stands for the present race-value of humanity, the Man in the midst of a world of relativity, alternation, pairs of opposites, etc.

We may give a significance to these numbers in terms of our daily life and experience, so that they shall answer to character and fortunes whenever they are applied to individuals. This has been done to some extent in the first part of this work, and may be here extended to cover particular cases which afford abnormal indications. Let us therefore presume that the following characteristics are those suited to the expression of the several numerical values :

Dignity	1	Pride.
Flexibility	2	Vacillation.
Generosity	3	Extravagance.
Practicality	4	Ostentation.
Discernment	5	Inquisitiveness.

Gentleness	6	Laxity.
Purpose	7	Prejudice.
Discretion	8	Timidity.
Zeal	9	Bigotry.

We shall then find that there are abnormal as well as normal characteristics to be accounted for. These abnormalities arise from the opposition of different planets, sets of vibrations, etc., and, as these have not been hitherto represented, they may be noticed in this place.

It should be observed, then, that numbers which enter into the enumeration of a birth-rate, as set forth in the Kabala of the Square of Three (*Kab.*, i. ch. iv.), and that are not brought into alliance by the interposition of another number, are said to be in opposition if in the same perpendicular or horizontal line.

Thus, to cite a particular instance, St Louis was born on the 23rd April 1215, and this by the Kabala is found to give the following Square of Three:

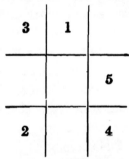

Sum = 6 Venus.

The sum is seen to respond to the value of Venus 6, which denotes gentleness. Also by the planetary conjunctions we find the Sun in conjunction with

Jupiter dominating the destiny and character.   But also there is the conjunction of Mercury and the Sun on the lower planes, which would enable the benevolent character of this monarch to find a practical expression.   So much was seen in the case as presented in the first part of our Kabala.

The oppositions represented here are those of Jupiter and the Moon and the Moon and Sun, since the Moon (2) and Jupiter (3) are in the same vertical line without an interposing and co-ordinating factor, which here should be Venus (6.)   Also the Moon (2) is in the same line with Sun (4), without the intervening number 8.

In Napoleon I.'s scheme we get oppositions of Sun and Saturn and Sun and Mars.   In Milton's scheme we have Sun opposition Saturn.   In Cagliostro's we find Sun opposition Mars.   In the case of Louis XVI. we find Moon opposition Jupiter, but no conjunction of Sun and Jupiter, as in the case of St Louis ; but, on the contrary, there are sinister conjunctions of Sun and Saturn and Moon and Saturn, which are absent from the data of the more fortunate monarch.

Similarly, there are trines formed between the planets by the fact of two numbers holding the extreme positions in the same line of a scheme with another holding a central position in another line. Thus, in the scheme of Napoleon I. (*Kab.*, i. p. 46), the numbers 9 and 4 are in the same line, and they form a triangle with 6 in another line.   Hence we have the trine of Mars and Venus, and also the Sun and Venus, on the base line of the opposition of Sun and Mars.   The same combination appears in the case of Cagliostro.   In the cases of both Louis XVI. and St Louis we have the triangle of 3–5–2—namely, Moon and Mercury, Mercury and Jupiter.   This is repeated in the case of Queen Victoria.

Therefore, from a variety of considerations which employ numbers as factors for the estimating of character and destiny, we may derive considerable information if we take these numbers as answering to the various planets of the system, regard them as incorporated in the date of birth, and then find their conjunctions, oppositions, and trines, and so make account of the results attributable to these inter-actions, taking the sum of the scheme to be indicative of the particular vibration to which the whole nature responds.

Thus, in the case of Charles, Duke of Bourbonnais, Constable of Bourbon, who was born on the 25th February 1489 (converted to new style), or 16th February, old style, we have the scheme as here shown :

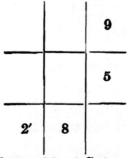

Sum = 26 = 8 Saturn.

Conjunctions.

Mars and Mercury.

Moon and Saturn.

Here the conjunction of Mars and Mercury indicated extreme mental activity and irascibility, while the Moon conjunct Saturn points to maiming and misfortune. The Key Number is of sinister import, answering as it does to the unit value of Saturn. There are no remedial trines. He was killed at the age of 38 by the bursting of a shell at the siege of Rome.

Lord Brougham had a very strong personality and a strongly set purpose, as is seen from the following scheme:

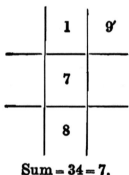

Sum = 34 = 7.

Conjunctions.

Sun and Mars.
Sun and Moon.
Moon and Saturn.

This is altogether lacking in the scheme of Charles II., which merely shows a complacent conjunction of Venus and Jupiter, indicating at best generosity and gentleness, with a material base of Saturn. This indication of the number 8 being repeated in the sum of the scheme, has a sinister import as regards material affairs.

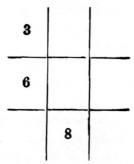

Sum, 17 = 8 Saturn.

Conjunction.
Jupiter and Venus.

It should be observed that the value of 4 is not the same as 5, though both apply to the Sun. But 1 has direct reference to character and 4 to material prosperity. Similarly, 7 and 2 are not to be regarded as having the same significance in a scheme, for 7 has relation to purpose and character, whereas 2 has reference to material change and circumstance. Thus the conjunction of Sun 4 and Saturn 8 has an entirely different value to a conjunction of Sun 1 and Saturn 8. In the first case there is material disaster, and in the other there is loss of reputation and honour.

It has been suggested that instead of taking the secular notation of the month of birth, as 1 for January, 2 February, etc., it would be more consistent to take the value of the planet ruling the sign in which the Sun is at the time. This while quite in line with the traditional methods of the Kabalists, will entail an inspection of the ephemeris, as there is a date in each month on which the Sun changes its sign, which is about the 20th of each month, though it differs by 1 to 3 days according to the month and year in question, owing to the difference between the secular months and the astronomical month.

Further, it would be in keeping with this scheme to take the actual day of the week on which a person was born and use the value of the planet ruling that day. Students should employ both these variants and observe which method gives the best results. It is admitted that there is no necessary connection between the secular dates and the characters and fortunes of those born thereon once we dismiss the idea of law and number as the governing factors in all manifestation. If, however, we see fit to adhere to these conceptions, unorthodox though they may be, we shall find occasion and reason for including all apparently chance happenings in the category of things related and designed.

For the purpose of comparing the systems of Kabala, however, it may be well to give the day and date numbers.

DAYS OF THE WEEK

The day of the week begins at noon for each day.
Sunday ruled by Sun—Number 1 when Sun is in
 a male or odd sign.
Number 4 when Sun is in female or even sign.

Monday—Number 7 when the Moon is in a Male
   sign.
   Number 2 when the Moon is in a female sign.
Tuesday—Number 9.
Wednesday—Number 5.
Thursday—Number 3.
Friday—Number 6.
Saturday—Number 8.

DAYS OF THE MONTH

January 1–20—ruled by Saturn—Number 8.

January 21–February 19 — ruled by Saturn —
Number 8.

February 20–March 19—ruled by Jupiter—
Number 3.

March 20–April 19—ruled by Mars—Number 9.

April 20–May 20—ruled by Venus—Number 6.

May 21–June 20—ruled by Mercury—Number 5.

June 21–July 22—ruled by Moon—Numbers 7
and 2.

July 23–August 22—ruled by Sun—Numbers
1 and 4.

August 23–September 22—ruled by Mercury—
Number 5.

September 23–October 22—ruled by Venus—
Number 6.

October 23–November 21—ruled by Mars—
Number 9.

November 22–December 21—ruled by Jupiter—
Number 3.

December 22–December 31—ruled by Saturn—
Number 8.

7

Note.—In June, July, and August female births take the number of the planet agreeing with the sex—namely, 2 for the Moon and 4 for the Sun. Male births take 7 for the Moon and 1 for the Sun.

This question being disposed of by the simple expedient of giving such building material as is required for the work, and letting everybody suit himself as to the particular style of architecture he fancies, we may pass on to the consideration of

Sound Values,

concerning which there is considerable dispute. This must inevitably be the case so long as you have dialectical differences. In the Hebrew evaluation there is no such difficulty, inasmuch as the Hebraic equivalent of every English letter is well known, and the values are applied irrespective of the phonetic value a letter may have in a word. Thus, by the Table of Hebraic Values (*Kab.*, i. p. 30), we have for the name Aboyeur (Fr.) $1271562 = 24 = 6$, and there is no doubt about it. But when we come to the Universal or Phonetic Values (*ibid.*), which I have said is the most satisfactory in its general application, we are faced by the difficulty that two persons may give different phonetic quantities to the same word. Thus, Aboyeur may be coded as 126162 (A-bo-yur), but a French-speaking student would code it 226112 (A'-bwah-yĕr), though the English transliteration does not quite convey it. The evaluation of the name in the one case is $18 = 9$, and in the other 14=5, and because 9 and 5 are taken in some systems as interchangeable, both would consider that they had coded it correctly.

A more difficult case would be the name of the Australian horse whose name is Urelia, 162131= 14=5 (U-reel-ya), but which the inconsequent pencillers converted by laying the stress on the penultimate, to which " You're another " appeared to be the only suitable reply.

Granted, however, that we are agreed as to our quantities, there is certainly no more satisfactory system of evaluation of names than the Phonetic. But, as I have always insisted, and here repeat, " Each system has to be employed in relation to its own method of interpretation," and to make no doubt of it, I have specifically cited two cases (*Kab.*, i. 30) : " The Hebrew method is employed for the kabalistic interpretation of the Scripture, as in the *Zohar*. It is especially suited to the Tarotic interpretation by the Twenty-two Major Keys "; and "The Pythagorean alphabet is used in connection with the interpretation employed in that system." There cannot, therefore, be any doubt in the matter. If people use one method of evaluation and another of interpretation and find there is no truth in it, the fault is with them and can be easily corrected.

It is, of course, possible to apply one's own evaluation, but more difficult to find a method of interpretation which fits it. Thus I have seen some curious results derived by the use of the decimal evaluation of the English alphabet :

A B C D E F G H I J
1 2 3 4 5 6 7 8 9
K L M N O P Q R S
1 2 3 4 5 6 7 8 9
T U V W X Y Z

and when the letters are taken in connection with the signs of the zodiac and applied to the names of competitors to know the result of a contest, the reading has been singularly curious.   In this scheme the letters fall thus :

Aries	Taurus	Gemini	Cancer	Leo	Virgo	Libra
AN	BO	CP	DQ	ER	FS	GT

Scorpio	Sagittarius	Capricornus	Aquarius	Pisces
HU	IJVW	KX	LY	MZ

The day being divided into 24 hours and counted from equatorial sunrise (which is 6 o'clock) to the time of an event, beginning with that planet and number which belongs to the day, as Moon 7 on Monday, Mars 9 on Tuesday, and so on, then that planet which coincides with the hour in which the event took place will, by its position in the zodiac, give a numerical value to every letter in the name of the winning competitor. These being computed and reduced to a unit value, they are found to correspond with the planetary number governing the hour in which the event took place.

But it will be found, upon examination, that however ingeniously we labour with such cypher alphabets we shall come no nearer than to note a certain correspondence between the values ascribed to the letters and the planet that happens to be in rotational order at the moment.

Far more significance attaches to the language of the heavens if only we are able to read it, and in such case it gives its message clearly and without ambiguity, neither is there need to make any calculation in the matter save to find what planet holds the greatest significance by chief position in the heavens at the time, as indeed some examples will readily show.

These " pointers," as we call them astrologically, doubtless depend upon the harmony of form, colour, name, and number that is seen to characterise the whole physiognomy of Nature, so that, while one may be intent upon discovering a ruling number, another will be searching for the prevailing colour, another for the dominant sound, and so forth, while the astrologer merely seizes on the general physiognomy of the case, taking the aspect of Nature at the moment, and finding in her at all times a revelation of some hidden truth. By way of illustration I may adduce the following few examples from among a large collection of others coming under my notice from time to time.

Mars being in the ascendant in its own sign Aries, being the only planet in its own sign at the time, "Rubra" (red) won a race from five competitors. Note that the planet Mars rules red.

The Moon exactly rising in the military sign Aries, "The White Knight" won from several competitors. Here Moon is " white " and Mars is " knight."

The Moon being in its own sign Cancer, and elevated above all the other bodies, " Cream of the Sky " won a conspicuous victory in quite unexpected form.

Mars being exactly on the Mid-heaven, and therefore the most notable feature of the celestial chart, " Rubio " won the Grand National Steeplechase at the remarkable price of 66 to 1 against.

These examples will sufficiently serve, no doubt, to indicate the extremely simple method of such observations. It amounts practically to the discernment of such correspondences as may exist in any particular instance. But in the nature of the case they are not always represented, and are sometimes difficult to recognise even where present. The student of occultism is, however, always on the look-out for such " pointers," even in the affairs of daily life.

CHAPTER VII

THE LAW OF PERIODICITY

IT has been shown, from a careful computation of factors involved, that as regards a pack of cards, a roulette wheel, and many other methods of employing the element of chance, a certain combination may be counted upon to recur at stated intervals; and although it cannot be shown that these intervals can be predicted, it can certainly be shown that they do recur within given limits.

But this is quite different from showing that particular factors are bound to recur at stated and predicable intervals, and, as this is my task, it will be seen that there can be only one way through, and that is by employing natural factors. For Nature undoubtedly has a periodicity which can be understood and anticipated.

Naturalists observe that certain habits of creatures are governed by the seasons, though they cannot say how the intelligence or instinct of those creatures can compass the vagaries of an English climate and yet strike true within - twenty-four hours, as may be observed in the migration of birds, the various periods of nesting and hatching, the

colonising of ants, the swarming of bees, and similar
natural phenomena apparently governed by instinct—an unknown quantity to human methods
of intelligence.

Astronomers also observe that there are cycles
and periods within which Nature repeats her
phenomena, from the rising of the sun to the
apparition of a comet. These observations submit
readily to a mathematical law, and the recurrence of
similar celestial phenomena are therefore predicable.
It is from this basis that I shall be able to demonstrate that matters apparently governed by chance
are subject to a like periodicity to that which we
observe in Nature, and for the reason that they, too,
are governed by natural laws.

Let us take two factors only as the ground of our
argument—the Sun and Moon. When these bodies
are conjoined in the heavens, so as to appear in the
same meridian at the same time, we get what are
called Spring Tides. The Sun and Moon are then
acting together on the same side of the earth, and
consequently the tides are highest. But when they
are acting from opposite sides of the earth, as at the
full moon, we get Neap Tides. Now, if there were
no interaction between the Sun, Moon, and Earth,
and if, further, there were no periodicity or regular
recurrence of their mutual relations, then we could
not construct a Tide-table such as forms part of our
annual almanacs. But this we can do for years and
decades in advance, so that the common formula
$t_{\frac{d}{2}}$ has a numerical significance which is quite
appreciable and has a constant value for the same

day of the Moon's age for every month in the
year.

To go a step further, let us suppose that the tidal
energy has an equivalent in regard to animate life,
as we find it to have in regard to the inanimate
waters of the globe.   Let us presume that it has a
subtle, although as yet undefined, action upon the
sap of plants, the juices and humours of animals,
and the blood-pressure of human beings.   And this,
when carefully thought over, is not presuming very
much, for it is certainly the fact that atmospheric
pressure is increased at the new and full of the Moon,
and that lunatics and feeble-minded persons respond
to increased blood-pressure at such times.   We call
them lunatics simply because they are subject to
this lunar influence.   The Sun maintains approximately the same relations with a given meridian at
the same time each day, but the Moon does not do
so, and it is to her variability that the gradual
recession of the tides upon a meridian is due.   For
if on a particular day the Sun and Moon are
conjoined, the next day will see the Sun at the same
hour in the same relations with the meridian, but
the Moon will be about 12° to the east, having
advanced about 13° in its apparent orbit, while the
Sun has only advanced 1°.   The following day the
Moon will be a further 12° east of the Sun, and so it
will continue until the two bodies are in opposition
and cross the meridian on opposite sides of the earth
at the same time.   The distance between the Moon
and Sun is called *Elongation*, *i.e.* longitude out of
the meridian which the Sun holds.   If we multiply

this distance or elongation by 4, we shall convert degrees of longitude into minutes of time, and this time will be the time after noon at which normal high tide is due at a place ; and this would actually be the time at which it happened but for local disturbing causes.   With these, however, we are not now concerned, and I only venture upon a popular explanation of the tides in order to establish the premiss of my argument, which is that the Moon as variable factor is what we must look to in connection with any periodicity we may hope to find in connection with apparently chance events.

Imagine a number of competitors in an event as having an equal chance of success.   Such, for example, is the idea aimed at in the process of handicapping by distance from " scratch," or by additional weight.   In the case of racehorses this is effected by allotting weight for age, plus penalties, or additional weights, for successive wins.   In effect we find that we are able to distinguish the competitors by the weights they carry, but we cannot distinguish the winner because the handicapping has given to each an equal chance.   Hence the grounds for speculation and wagering which is a feature of all such contests, " the spice in the pudding," as its advocates affirm.

By a comparative study of various records, I find that I am able to present the net results of my investigations in a single glyph which, from what has been said, will doubtless be appreciable by the intelligent reader.

The fact is that one may triangulate upon any series of events of like nature with an absolute certainty of gaining a majority of them by as many as seven in every ten, or seventy per cent., and that by no further trouble than is involved in the study of the tidal law we have been considering.   It will be observed that the circle or sphere of action is divided by interlaced triangles into 12 arcs of 30°

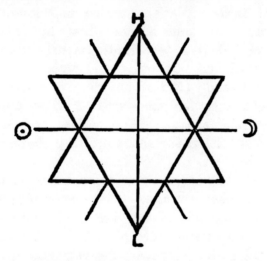

each, three being included in each quadrant of the circle.   Then two divisions will equal 60°, and this gives us 6 in the circle, and $42 \div 6 = 7$, which is therefore due to each of the arcs between ⊙ and H, H and ☽, L and ⊙, L and ☽.   So that in taking the relations of the three factors into account and applying the tidal law, we arrive at a periodicity of results that have a direct weight relation to one another.   An exposition of this law would occupy a great deal of space and would usurp the main

purpose of this work.   I have therefore only hinted
at the method of procedure.

But as soon as we come to the study of sound
values, *i.e.* the numerical value of vibrations, we
are able to exemplify this law of periodicity in a
simple and convincing manner.   This statement,
however, involves the fact of such phonetic values
having cosmic equivalents, and hence that the
planets are linked up with number and sound as
well as colour in such manner that by tracing
planetary periods we are simultaneously tracing
their numerical and phonetic correlatives.   This, I
endeavoured to show (*Kab.*, i. ch. viii.), was actually
the fact, and I so far succeeded as to stimulate
inquiry for further examples, illustrations, and rules,
and, as this is within the scheme of my chapter, I
may do so here.

It was seen that the basis of our calculation was
the Sun's true centre rising.   This means that the
astronomical longitude of the Sun is rising on the
celestial horizon of the place for which calculation
is made.   On p. 85, however, the rule was trans-
posed in error.   The ascensional difference of the
Sun must be *added* to 90° when the Sun's declination
is *North*, and *subtracted* when it is *South* ; and the
result multiplied by 4 will give the minutes in time
before noon at which the Sun rose.   The example
on p. 86 is worked correctly and will serve as a
guide.   It should be remarked, however, that the
rule should be reversed for places South of the
Equator, as for Australia, New Zealand, etc.,
and the ascensional difference *added* when the

Sun's declination is South, and *subtracted* when North.

In order to prove the periodicity of numerical values and their sound equivalents, we have only to take two consecutive days and show that the same unit values are in force at corresponding times, *i.e.* at times when the planetary periods are the same ; or, alternatively, we may take two consecutive Wednesdays, or Thursdays, and show the same results from the same or equivalent times. Let us take two consecutive days.

Newmarket—Wednesday, April 17th, 1912. Lat. 52° 15′ N. ⊙'s declin. N = 10° 21′.

To find the Sun's ascn. difference, add together the logarithms of the tangents of 52° 15′ and 10° 21′. Thus :

$$
\begin{array}{lll}
\text{Log. tan. } 52°\ 15' & & 10\text{·}11110 \\
\quad\text{„}\quad\text{„}\quad 10°\ 21' & & 9\text{·}26158 \\
\hline
\quad\text{„}\quad \text{sine } 13°\ 38\tfrac{1}{2}' & = & 9\text{·}37268
\end{array}
$$

These logarithms will be found in Chambers's Mathematical Tables. The sum of the two logs. gives us the log. sine of the Sun's ascensional difference, and, as the declination is N. and the latitude of place N., we must add 13° 38½′ to 90° and multiply by 4 in order to find the time before noon at which the Sun rose on Newmarket.

Thus, 90° + 13° 38½′ = 103° 38½′

$$
\begin{array}{r}
103°\ 38\tfrac{1}{2}' \\
4 \\
\hline
414^m\ 34^s = 6^h\ 54^m\ 34^s
\end{array}
$$

Hence the local time of sunrise was 5.5 a.m.
nearly, and the corresponding Greenwich time would
be 5.4 a.m.

The Sun will be 6^h 55^m coming from the horizon to
the meridian, and the same time, approximately,
from meridian to sunset. We are only concerned
with the afternoon of April 17th, and so we take the
semiarc of the Sun from noon to setting, viz.
6^h 55^m, and divide this by 6 to get the length of the
planetary hour = 1^h 9^m nearly. As there are 6
planetary hours from sunrise to noon, the seventh
hour will begin at noon, and the Horary Speculum
(*Kab.*, i. p. 84) tells us that on Wednesday the
seventh hour is ruled by Venus and the eighth by
Mercury. Each " hour " is at this date 1^h 9^m in
length, and therefore Venus will rule from noon to
1.9 p.m., and Mercury will begin at 1.9 p.m. and
continue to rule till 2.18 p.m.

But each hour is subdivided into seven parts, and
each of these sub-periods is ruled successively by
the planets in rotation. Then to find the length of
each sub-period divide 1^h 9^m by seven, which is 10^m
nearly. With these preliminary calculations we
can set out the Table for the day, showing the
beginnings of the hours or periods, and also those of
the sub-periods, for Wednesday, April 17th, 1912.
It will be observed that the 8th sub-period, which
would be ruled by the same planet as that which
governs the hour, syncopates in this scheme, and
is replaced by the planet governing the next hour
and sub-period in succession. Otherwise the
Chaldean order is in every respect observed, thus:

Wednesday, April 17, 1912

Venus 12·0		Mercury 1·9		Moon 2·18		Saturn 3·27		Jupiter 4·36		Mars 5·45	
♀	12·0	☿	1·9	☽	2·18	♄	3·27	♃	4·36	♂	5·45
☿	12·10	☽	1·19	♄	2·28	♃	3·37	♂	4·46	☉	5·55
☽	12·20	♄	1·29	♃	2·38	♂	3·47	☉	4·56	♀	6·5
♄	12·30	♃	1·39	♂	2·48	☉	3·57	♀	5·6	☿	6·15
♃	12·40	♂	1·49	☉	2·58	♀	4·7	☿	5·16	☽	6·25
♂	12·50	☉	1·59	♀	3.8	☿	4·17	☽	5·26	♄	6·35
☉	1·0	♀	2·9	☿	3·18	☽	4·27	♄	5·36	♃	6·45
♀		☿		☽		♄		♃		♂	

The Speculum ends with the period of Mars and the sub-period of Jupiter, and this latter extends for 10^m, which brings us to 6.55, the time of sunset. Now the events of the day were as follows—

2.0	Won by Kempion	=	214825	=4	☉
2.30	„ Thimble filly	=	9423831	=3	♃
3.0	„ Saracen	=	6121615	=4	☉
3.30	„ Jackdaw	=	31242	=3	♃
4.0	„ Clay Pigeon	=	231835	=4	☉
4.30	„ Pintadeau	=	854146	=1	☉
5.0	„ Thunderstone	=9254126465		=8	♄

At first sight it may not appear that all these results are in harmony with our law. Let us, however, examine them. The first event at 2.0 falls in sub-period of the Sun = 4 negative, and is won by Kempion = 4.

At 2.30, ruled by Saturn, number 3 wins. We should have expected 1 or 8 to win. But on reference we find Saturn at this date in Taurus, ruled by Venus, whose negative number is 3 (*Kab.*, i. p. 90). We are here dealing with the afternoon, which is negative, and therefore look for negative numbers.

At 3.0, ruled by Sun, Saracen wins in correct time ; Sun = 4 negative.

At 3.30, ruled by Saturn, Jackdaw = 3 won. The same result as for 2.30, where Saturn, in sign of Venus negative = 3, was replaced by 3.

At 4.0, ruled by Sun, Clay Pigeon = 4 wins.

At 4.30, ruled by Moon, Pintadeau = 1 wins. Here the Moon is in Taurus and 3 should win.

At 5.0, ruled by Sun, Thunderstone = 8 wins. This being the number of Saturn, it is alternate to the Sun. There were no less than five competitors of value 1 = Sun positive, but none value 4, and in consequence the Sun wins under 8.

Therefore we find that out of seven events four are direct and unequivocal, being won by horses whose names are phonetic equivalents of the negative ruling number of the periods in which they won. Two others are won by the negative number of the planet in whose sign the ruler of the period is found at the time.

But, generally, it will be found that the events which do not fall into line with the law are won by the number represented by the sign the Moon is in. On April 17 it was just entering Taurus=3. This is invariably the case when the ☽ is the sub-period planet and there is no number 2 present among the competitors.

For convenience of those who have no astrological knowledge I here give the negative values of the signs of the zodiac.

NEGATIVE NUMBERS OF THE SIGNS.

♈	♉	♊	♋	♌	♍	♎	♏	♐	♑	♒	♓
5	3	9	2	4	9	3	5	6	1	1	6

Now let us take the next day, April 18th. The Sun's declin. being 10° 42' log. tan.   9·27635
                Lat.   52° 15'   ,,   ,,   10·11110
                                        _____

    Asc. diff. 14° 7½'   ,,   sine   9·38745
        +90° 0'
    _____

        104° 7½'
             4
    _____

    416° 30' =6ʰ 56ᵐ 30ˢ.

The period from noon to sunset is thus seen to be 6ʰ 56½ᵐ, which, divided by 6, gives the *period* of 1ʰ 9ᵐ 10ˢ; and this, again, divided by 7 gives the *sub-period* of 10ᵐ nearly.

8

The events were as follows :—

1.0	—Shipshape	$38318 = 23 = 5.$
1.30	—Biter Bit	$2142\ 24 = 15 = 6.$
2.0	—Thrace	$9216 = 18 = 9.$
2.30	—Jingling Geordie	$352352\ 32241 = 32 = 5.$
3.0	—Distcha	$4631 = 14 = 5.$
3.30	—Tullibardine	$423212415 = 24 = 6.$

At 1.0 the period was just changing from Mercury to Moon, and, allowing 1 minute for east longitude of Newmarket, there was 1 minute of Mercury's period to expire at the set time of the race. Consequently we find Shipshape = 5 winning under its own number. This is irregular if a 9 was present, but it is not in contravention of the law.

At 1.30 the Sun was ruling, and he was on this date in Taurus, ruled by Venus, who won under its own number 6.

At 2.0 the Moon was ruling. 9 won, this being contrary to our rule, but in agreement with the suggestion that Mars is the alternate to the Moon (*Cosmic Symbolism*).

At 2.30 the Sun was ruling. Here the Sun in Taurus = 3, and Geordie = 3, but the full name = 5, a misfit.

At 3.0 the Moon was ruling. Winner = 5. See above where Mars (negative 5) wins in same period.

At 3.30 the Sun again rules in Taurus = 3, but the positive number 6 wins.

The results, though involved, are mainly in support of the theory we have adopted. Taken over a period, the findings are abundantly satisfac-

tory. But this, of course, is not advanced as a
system of selection. At best, and like all other
systems depending on name values, it is a system of
exclusion, or what is called in science a method of
exhaustion. I presume it would be impossible to
formulate any law which does not admit of ex-
ceptions, because our laws are founded upon
observation of the direct working of one form of
energy, and this may be interfered with by the
operation and interaction of other forms of energy,
whether by resistance or by deflection.

A method for employing the positive numbers
of the planets may here be mentioned. It is
based on the Hebraic view that the day com-
mences at noon and not at sunrise, as is generally
and erroneously believed. The statement in
Genesis is, "The evening and the morning were
the first day." Not by any stretch of fancy
could we speak of the period from sunrise to
sunset as "the evening," nor from sunset to sunrise
as "morning." But we can quite legitimately
refer to the period from noon to midnight as "the
evening," and from midnight to noon as "the
morning."

The planet giving its name to the day takes rule
over the first hour after noon, and is followed in the
Chaldean order by the other planets, and so on in
rotation. Each hour is taken as 60^m in length, and
is subdivided into 15 parts of 4 minutes each, the
first of which is ruled by the planet of the day, and
followed by the rest in rotation. Thus Sunday is
divided as follows :

Noon to 1 p.m. Sun
1 p.m. to 2   „   Venus
2   „   to 3   „   Mercury
3   „   to 4   „   Moon
4   „   to 5   „   Saturn
5   „   to 6   „   Jupiter
etc., etc.

Then the hour of Venus, from 1 to 2 p.m., will divide into sub-periods thus:

1☉, 2♀, 3☿, 4☽, 5♄, 6♃, 7♂, 8☉, 9♀, 10☿, 11☽, 12♄, 13♃, 14♂, 15☉.

The planet ruling the day, that ruling the hour, and that ruling the sub-period, are represented by their positive numbers, and these being added together, the sum is reduced to its unit value. The winner of a race or contest taking place in the limits of the sub-period should have a name which is the phonetic equivalent of the unit value of the three factors.

The Tables of the Hours and sub-periods of the week, counted from noon each day, are as follows:

Sunday	.	1657839	recurring
Monday	.	7839165	„
Tuesday	.	9165783	„
Wednesday	.	5783916	„
Thursday	.	3916578	„
Friday	.	6578391	„
Saturday	.	8391657	„
Hours .	.	1234567	from noon
Periods .	.	1234567	from Hour

Example : 11 Sept. 1911—Saturday.

 Saturday = 8
 3rd hour = 9
 1st period = 8
    ———

    25 = 7, won by Countess Mac = 9.
Suggested alternative of Moon 7 = Mars 9.

 Saturday = 8
 3rd hour = 9
 8th period = 8
    ———

    25 = 7, won by Holt's Pride = 2.
Negative ☽ period = 2.

 Saturday = 8
 4th hour = 1
 1st period = 8
    ———

    17 = 8, won by Chasuble = 4.

 Saturday = 8
 4th hour = 1
 8th period = 8
    ———

    17 = 8, won by Cylgad = 8.

 Saturday = 8
 5th hour = 6
 1st period = 8
    ———

    22 = 4, won by Montmartre = 8.

Saturday   = 8
5th hour   = 6
8th period = 8
----
22 = 4, won by Wolftoi = 8.

The Coding used is as follows :
Countess Mac   225416 412 = 27 = 9.
Holt's Pride   563468 24 = 38 = 11 = 2.
Chasuble   317623 = 22 = 4.
Cylgad   613214 = 17 = 8.
Montmartre   425241242 = 26 = 8.
Wolftoi   6238421 = 26 = 8.

Thus it will be seen that, with the exception of the first event, all the results are in harmony with our customary evaluations, and support the scheme here for the first time advanced. In the first case it is of interest to note that the Moon 7 was, on 11 September 1911, in the sign Aries, ruled by Mars 9 ; and this fact appears to support the general ascription of " variability " applied to the Moon. Certainly it is repeatedly observed that the Moon can win in any period whose mass value (as above) agrees with the planet ruling the sign it is in, as follows :

♈	♉	♊	♋	♌	♍	♎	♏	♐	♑	♒	♓
9	6	5	2	4	5	6	9	3	8	8	3
			7	1							

Some little while ago I instituted a test with an old student of the " Mysteries of Sound and Number," a man whose patience and faculty for figures were backed by a considerable knowledge of turf matters. In making selections before the event and using the above system called "Trilogia," because it employs three arguments, it was found that I could easily double his successes, after making my selections in half the time. The reasons for this superiority were that I had not to speculate on the " off " time, but merely to use the set time of the event ; that I had not to take any count of the distance to be run; and, finally, that my method of coding was simpler than his. But probably the chief reason lay in the fact that he was never correct in his times of sunrise except for places in or about the same latitude as Greenwich— and fortunately for him, and the system he followed, these included Bath, Salisbury, Windsor, Gatwick, Epsom, Kempton Park, Hurst Park, Alexandra Park, Ascot, Bibury, Brighton, Folkestone, Lewes, Goodwood, Lingfield, Sandown Park, and Newbury. This was the broad base on which an astounding fallacy was erected, and when we came to deal with Liverpool, Manchester, York, Newcastle, Ayr, and some other northern centres, the record he had been building in the South went to pieces.

We may now look at the subject of periodicity from another point of view.

CHAPTER VIII

PERIODICITY OF EVENTS

IN trying to trace a law of periodicity in regard to things of chance which apparently have but small significance in the main purpose of human life, and yet which, being included, must in some way be conformable to the general plan and subject to universal laws, we may find ourselves forced to rely upon partial and sporadic successes. We may assume a broader base with more certainty of success. It is easier to indicate which way the wind is blowing on the open plains than to take our reading from the play of some little eddy in the byways of a town. Consequently, when we come to the study of the law of periodicity in relation to the broad facts of history, we find that the indications are more marked and easier to discern. We take our pointers from the same cosmic factors that have guided our investigations from the first, and trace in the mutations of the planets certain definite changes in human affairs. From like causes we argue like effects, and the fact that these effects are repeatedly observable serves not only to confirm the validity of our argument, but also enables us to establish a law of periodicity in regard to events which, if they were not disposed by superior causes, would not respond to this law, being apparently under human control.

We have already seen that Mars represents energy, executiveness, and when vitiated its abnormal expression is seen to be violence, strife, and lawlessness. Normally it denotes freedom, abnormally it indicates licence. Saturn we have found to be associated with the number 8, which indicates destruction, revolution, inversion. One is a positive planet and the other a negative. The two acting together produce outbreaks of public feeling, violence, and mortality.

Elsewhere it will be seen that the sign of the zodiac ruling England is Aries, governed by Mars, and responding to the vibrations of the number 9 and the colour red. The popular expression " the all-red " refers very aptly to the British. By some play of human faculty this has been sensed and identified with all that is British, and accordingly we find our atlas showing the Empire extending across the two hemispheres all red. Therefore we may expect that Mars stirs up strife in various countries as it passes through the signs of the zodiac governing them, and that its conjunction with Saturn in the sign ruling a country is of sinister import. We find it so, in fact. Thus there was a conjunction of Saturn and Mars in Aries in 1879, and there followed the terrible Afghan and Zulu Wars. Passing into Taurus (ruling Ireland) the planets produced the agrarian outrages in

Ireland. In 1883 the conjunction fell in Gemini (ruling Lower Egypt), and was at once followed by the Soudan War and the tragedy of Khartoum. We might trace the whole circle of the zodiac, did space permit, until we come to the conjunction of these planets in Aquarius (ruling Russia) in 1904, and again in 1905, which brought about the defeat of Russia by the Japanese and the outburst of popular feeling which culminated in the disgraceful tragedy of " Red Sunday " ; and finally in Pisces, which brought Portugal into startling prominence by the assassination of the King and Crown Prince, and the Revolution which followed it.

Thus we come to 1909–10 and the destructive Socialist policy of the Lloyd-George clique, the Dock and Coal Strikes, the War scare of 1912, and the Suffragette outrages. From 1879 to 1909 is a period of thirty years, which is approximately the period of this conjunction as regards any part of the zodiac. If we go back thirty years from 1879 we come to 1849 and the Sikh War. A second conjunction followed in 1851, and was soon followed by the Russian War. Its immediate effect was the *coup d'état* of Louis Napoleon and the jeopardising of British interests by his ambitions. Then we go back thirty years and find Saturn and Mars again in Aries in the year 1821, which was the period of the Cato Street Conspiracy and the suicide of Lord Londonderry (Lord Castlereagh), then Minister of State for Foreign Affairs.

So that whether we trace this combination of Mars and Saturn (9+8) through the successive signs

at intervals of two years, or from one conjunction to the next in the same sign at intervals
of thirty years, we find its effects disturbing and
destructive.

But we may take the cycle of 265 years, which
admits of many minor cycles, and we find the same
planets conjoined in exactly the same part of the
zodiac. Thus from the epoch 1909–10 it brings
us to 1644 and the overthrow of the Royalists at
Marston Moor. Then from 1644 we take the cycle
again and come to 1379 and the Rebellion under
Wat Tyler. From that date we go back to 1114,
when England was disturbed by the wars waged
by Henry I. against Robert of Bêlleme and France.
Going a further cycle back, to 849, we come to the
Danish invasion during the reign of Egbert. Prior
to this epoch history becomes obscure in regard to
British affairs, and so we may leave it. The cycle
has been traced in regard to other countries ruled
by other signs than Aries, and undoubtedly we
have complete evidence of a connected periodicity
of events due to the combined action of these two
major planets.

Conjunctions of Saturn and Jupiter lead to great
mutations in those countries ruled by the signs in
which the conjunctions fall. The conjunctions
differ from those of Mars and Saturn in this respect,
that whereas the latter pass regularly through the
signs at intervals of about two years, those of Saturn
and Jupiter remain in the same triplicity for several
decades. At present they are in the earthy triplicity,
embracing the signs of Taurus, Virgo, and Capri-

corn, and have been so since 1842. Every twenty
years these planets are conjoined in one of these
signs—namely, in 1842, Capricorn; 1861–2, Virgo;
1881, Taurus ; 1901, Capricorn ; 1921, Virgo ; 1941,
Taurus ; 1961, Capricorn ; 1981, Libra. Thus we
get a change of triplicity after seven periodic
conjunctions. Hence, from 1842 to 1981, the
countries ruled by the earthy trigon—among which
are India, New Zealand, Greece, Turkey, Mexico,
Ireland, and Persia—experience great mutations.
These mutations are eventually of good effect, and
always lead to a beneficial legislation and the
establishment of a more solid constitution. After
1981 the conjunction will begin to affect Japan,
Russia, America, and Egypt. But, so far as history
serves us at this date, we find the countries named
to be among those whose affairs of state since 1842
have undergone most remarkable changes, and
further developments are likely to take place before
the cycle is completed. It will be seen that the
Indian Mutiny followed the conjunction in Capricorn, India's ruling sign ; that the Russian invasion
of Turkey, involving British interests, took place
after the conjunction in Virgo ; and the Coercion
Act, the Parnell agitation, the agrarian outrages,
and murder of Lord Frederick Cavendish (the
Secretary of State for Ireland), took place immediately upon the conjunction in Taurus. Minor
causes, the interplay of cycles according to periodic
law, at times retard, and at others accelerate, the
course of events ; but in the end the major influence
asserts itself and brings about those great convul-

sions in human thought and polity which we have been considering.

There are other features of this periodic law which depend on numerical sequences (*Kab.*, i. 71, 133). Some illustration of these has been given in the *Manual of Occultism*. What are called the fatal periods recur after a certain interval of years, depending on the radix. These are such as make the unit value of 13 and 16. The sequence is derived from the addition to any radical date of its own unit value, as 1870 = 16, which, being added to 1870, gives 1886 = 23, and this is repeating continuously. Thus Napoleon I. was born in 1769, and his numerical sequence would therefore be :

$$1769 = 23 \quad \text{Birth number.}$$
$$\underline{23}$$
$$1792 \qquad \text{The Revolution.}$$
$$\underline{23}$$
$$1815 \qquad \text{Waterloo.}$$

Another and more general sequence is this :

$$1769 = 23$$
$$\underline{23}$$
$$1792 = 19$$
$$\underline{19}$$
$$1811 = 11$$

The year 1811 corresponds with the turn of the tide in Napoleon's fortunes, for in that year Wellington made his first victory over the French in the Peninsula, and followed it up at Badajoz. Napoleon attained his 46th year in 1815, and this brings out:

$$
\begin{array}{r}
1815 \\
46 \\
\hline
1861 = 16
\end{array}
$$

the fatal number, which kabalistically answers to " The Stricken Tower " (*Kab.*, i. p. 29).

Other illustrations, taking as radix the founding of a dynasty or some great epoch in the history of a nation, will be found in my previous works.   The accession of George I. to the throne of Great Britain and the establishment of the Hanoverian dynasty in 1714 yields by numerical sequences the years 1727, 1744, 1760, 1774, 1793, and 1813 ; corresponding with the accession of George II., the Stuart Rebellion, the accession of George III., the American Rebellion, the French Revolution, and the Grand Alliance.   The Fall of Napoleon, 1815, gives 1830, Fall of Charles X., and this latter is derived also directly from the Fall of Robespierre in 1794. Shelley's career shows a curious periodicity by numerical sequence.

He was born $\begin{array}{l} 1792 = 19 \\ 19 \\ \hline 1811 \quad \text{Expelled from Oxford.} \\ 11 \\ \hline 1822 \quad \text{Expelled from the world.} \end{array}$

Here, again, the year 1822 is seen to have the unit
value of 13, "The Reaping Skeleton = Death," while
the age of thirty years, attained in 1822, gives 1852
= 16, "The Stricken Tower." All subjects do not
respond to the same kabalism, but all are subjects
of some periodicity in the course of events, and
frequently it will be found that, instead of the birth
date, we have to take this of the first great event,
and in my own case I find:

$$1868= \quad \begin{array}{l} 1868 \quad \text{Death of father.} \\ \underline{23} \\ 1891 \quad \text{Death of mother.} \end{array}$$

The House of Brunswick came to the British
throne in the person of King William IV., from
which we have the events:

$$1830 = 12 \quad \text{Accession of William IV.}$$
$$\underline{12}$$

$$1842 = 15 \quad \text{Scinde War.}$$
$$\underline{15}$$

$$1857 = 21 \quad \text{Indian Mutiny.}$$
$$\underline{21}$$

$$1878 = 24 \quad \text{Afghan War.}$$
$$\underline{24}$$

$$1902 = 11 \quad \text{Accession of Edward VII.}$$
$$\text{Boer War ended.}$$
$$\underline{11}$$

$$1913 = 14 \quad \text{Balkan War and (?).}$$

The founding of the German Empire after the war with France in 1871 seems to lead to the same epoch, thus :

> 1871   German Empire.
>   17
> ———
> 1888   Accession of Kaiser Wilhelm III.
>   25
> ———
> 1913   (as above.)

Peter I. ascended the throne of Servia in 1903 = 13 — "Death, the Reaper," according to the Tarot. It was not until 1912 that this number recurred in the date, and then the Balkan War broke out. The horoscope is of interest :—

29 June 1844—morning = 28—6—44.

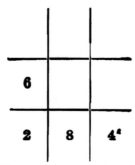

Sum, 24 = 6, Venus.

Conjunctions.

Moon and Venus.
Moon and Saturn.
Saturn and Sun.

It is an unfortunate scheme, and we may therefore expect that Servia will not come out well from the mêlée in the Balkans.

The Kabalists have cycles of 15, 34, 65, 111, 175, 260, and 369 years, which are the cycles of Saturn, Jupiter, Mars, Sun, Venus, Mercury, and the Moon respectively. An example of the constitutional effect of the Sun's period is seen in the case of Ireland :

1801   The Union.

111   Cycle of Sun.

———

1912   The Separation.

The Kabalists further divide the periods and also extend them, in the following manner :

Saturn	3,	9,	15,	45	years.
Jupiter	4,	16,	34,	136	,,
Mars	5,	25,	65,	325	,,
Sun	6,	36,	111,	666	,,
Venus	7,	49,	175,	1225	,,
Mercury	8,	64,	260,	2080	,,
Moon	9,	81,	369,	3321	,,

It will be observed that the sum of the least years of all the planets is 42, our gravity standard applied to the three triangles, or trilogia (ch. vii.). The sums of all the years are multiples of seven, namely, 6 times, 40 times, 147 times, and 1114 times. The periods differ from the astrological periods of the planets according to the Chaldeans, the values of these being :

For the Moon		4	years.
	Mercury	10	„
	Venus	8	„
	Sun	19	„
	Mars	15	„
	Jupiter	12	„
	Saturn	30	„

The Kabalists, however, extract the values of the planets from these periods, giving to Saturn 6, Jupiter 7, Mars 2, Sun 3, Venus 4, Mercury 8, and the Moon 9, as radical numbers, and they are used for the evaluation of names according to the Hebraic system. By kabalistic progression the further key numbers of the planets are derived, viz. Saturn 8, Jupiter 3, Moon 7, Mercury 5, Mars 9, Sun 4, Venus 6, which, as will be seen, are the numbers already and frequently associated with them by Haydon and others, the peculiar feature being that the Sun's negative number 4 and the Moon's positive number 7 are alone employed for those bodies.

The astronomical period of 19 years ascribed by the Chaldeans to the Sun has a close connection with the periodicity of events, because every 19 years the Sun and Moon form their phases on, or close to, the same date ; and as the recession of the Moon's nodes has a period of about 19 years also, it follows that there are two or three successive eclipses of the same kind in the same longitude at intervals of 19 years. Thus, there was an eclipse of the Sun on January 22nd, 1860, in ♒ 2°, another in 1879, January 22nd, in ♒ 2°, another in 1898, January 22nd, in ♒ 2°, the difference being in their respective magnitudes. From time immemorial eclipses have been regarded as significant portents in human affairs, and their symbolical value may readily be conceded, while as physical phenomena eclipses have recently received considerable attention from men of science, it having been conclusively shown that definite physical effects have followed immediately upon the obscuration of the luminary, more particularly in those parts where the eclipse was visible, and especially where it was vertical at the time of central conjunction. It is in the symbolical sense that we regard eclipses, and this because there is a periodicity attaching to their zodiacal position which is not observed in regard to any geographical locality. This period of 19 years has been observed since the days of Meton in the fifth century B.C. as of astrological value, that is, as a means of prognosis. Ptolemy and other of the early astronomers accede this symbolic value. Kepler confirmed it by his own observations, and suggested the regulation of human affairs as being effected by means of the celestial bodies. Be that as it may, the case should be capable of proof. Take, for instance, the large solar eclipse which happened over Europe on April 17th, 1912, in ♈ 27°. It was central in latitude 43° N., and its longitude from ♈0 was 27°. In longitude 27° East, and latitude 43° N., the Balkan War broke out, the significant fact being that ♂ Mars, on the very day, 14th October 1912, was in ♎ 27°, and therefore in exact opposition to the place of the eclipse. The war ran its course, and came to an end. The Allies well knew that the intervention of the Powers was merely a moral one, and that any attempt to police the situation would be very dangerous to the Power that undertook the work ; so they fought on, despite the protests of the Powers, and Turkey capitulated. But Roumania, who had taken an active part in the Alliance, was apparently to be shelved when the partition of territory came to be discussed. So it happened that in June 1913, when Mars was in transit over the place of eclipse in ♈ 27°, the war broke out again between the Allies themselves. Roumania speedily reduced Bulgaria and took the foremost position in the theatre of war, thus reversing the entire position and setting Europe at defiance. Here we see that a significant eclipse falling over Europe brings trouble upon that part of the world, and that the opening dates of the two great contests coincide exactly with the position of the martial planet Mars on the line of that eclipse.

As regards individuals, it has been found by long observation that events are repetitive in nature and sequence after 19 years in certain cases, as when the eclipses fall on significant points in the horoscope of a person's birth. Otherwise they are not so. King Edward VII. was born when the 26th degree of Sagittarius was rising. There were solar eclipses in this degree of the opposite sign Gemini in June 1852, 1871, 1890, and 1909. They were followed by unfortunate periods, and finally by death, as predicted, in the year 1910, within a year of the last of the series of eclipses. In other cases it is found that half the period of Saturn = 15 years, which alone is the whole period of Mars, has a sinister significance and recurs from the year in which Saturn transits a significator in the horoscope.

The study of planetary periods in the symbolical sense leads to a curious numerical fact which evidently has a significance in regard to the periodic law. If we place the Chaldean period of the planets in the order of the apparent velocity of the planets, thus :

Saturn	Jupiter	Mars	Venus	Mercury	Moon
30	12	5	8	10	4

and divide them into their least common multiple, 120, we shall get:

4	10	8	15	12	30

the same values in reverse order. Now, as 120 is the whole period of the planetary cycle according to both the Chaldean and Indian systems of astrology, we may see here a definite relationship of periods to polarities. For Saturn and the Moon are opposed to one another in respect of their signs Capricorn and Cancer ; Jupiter and Mercury in respect of their signs Sagittarius, Gemini and Pisces, Virgo ; Mars and Venus in respect of their signs Aries, Libra and Scorpio, Taurus (*Kab.*, i. p. 81). Then, if the circle of 120 years responds to the circle of 360°, it follows that the periods answering to the aspects 45°, 90°, 135°, 180°, which are regarded as malefic, being formed upon the cross, namely, the 15th, 30th, 45th, 60th, 75th, 90th, and 105th years of life are adversely climacteric. On the other hand, the years of life which answer to the aspects 60°, 120°, which are benefic, being formed on the triangle, namely, the 20th, 40th, 80th, and 100th years are favourable climacterics.   But inasmuch as individual births do not coincide with zero, but persons are born in all periods during the course of 120 years, the periods will not respond to individuals at the same ages, but at different ages according to the period in which they were born. This idea lies at the root of the 120-year cycle of the Indian Dasabukthi system.

If we deal with the numbers of the planets in the same way as with their periods, we get the basis in the unit series :—

0	1	2	3	4	5	6	7	8	9
✳	☉	☽	♃	☉	☿	♀	☽	♄	♂
+	−		−				+		

By adding the first and last, $0+9$, we get Mars $= 9$, $1+8=9$, $2+7=9$, $3+6=9$, $4+5=9$; and here we find Sun and Saturn, Jupiter and Venus in combination, the positive and negative Moon numbers $2+7=9$, and finally the negative Sun number 4 paired with the number of Mercury, which elsewhere (*Cosmic Symbolism*) has been suggested as the alternate of the Sun negative. On this point we shall have something more to say when we come to the practical application of these values.

CHAPTER IX

COINCIDENCES MAKE LAWS

THE method of finding sunrise, and hence the planetary hours and their sub-divisions, has already been given, and it will be found upon examination that many remarkable effects attach to the rulership of the planets during these periods. But very frequently it will be found that the planet ruling the day, or its zodiacal alternative, will take possession of and rule the whole day. One or two illustrations of this will not be without interest, and may possibly lead to further research along profitable lines.

The planet ♃ Jupiter rules on Thursday and gives its name to the day. Its zodiacal alternative is Mercury, so called because it rules the opposite zodiacal signs to Jupiter. Thus :

♃ rules ♐ and ♓ Number 3
☿ ,, ♊ ,, ♍ ,, 5

15th August 1912, fell on a Thursday. The following events took place at Kempton :

2.0 won by Dutch Courage = 46428 2762135 = 50 = 5.
2.30 ,,   ,, Jocasta = 3721341 = 21 = 3.
3.0 ,,   ,, Iron Duke = 1275 4625 = 32 = 5.
3.30 ,,   ,, Lomond = 374754 = 30 = 3.
4.0 ,,   ,, Drawbridge = 4216221435 = 30 = 3.
4.30 ,,   ,, Mesmer = 453452 = 23 = 5.

It will be seen that the Hebraic values are used for the evaluation of the names, and that all the events are under Jupiter or Mercury, values 3 and 5.

12th August, Monday, at Nottingham.

2.0 won by Artist's Song = 12413433752 = 35 = 8.
2.30 ,,   ,, Irish Demon = 121545475 = 34 = 7.
3.0 ,,   ,, Katanga = 2141521 = 16 = 7.
3.30 ,,   ,, Brancepeth = 2215258553 = 5 = 8,
4.0 ,,   ,, Translucence = 421533625525 = 43 = 7.
4.30 ,,   ,, Grave Greek = 32165 32552 = 34 = 7.

Here the values are those of the Moon 7 and Saturn 8, these planets being the ruler of the day and its zodiacal alternate respectively. The Moon rules ♋ Cancer, and Saturn rules the opposite sign ♑ Capricorn. It will be observed that the hard final in " song " is value 2, not 3 as when soft in such words as courage, drawbridge, etc. Also that the final *th*, as in Brancepeth, is of value 5, while *sh* in Irish is of value 5, *i.e.* $s = 6$ and $h = 8 = 14 = 5$, while the pure S sound is of value 3.

Thus on Tuesday, 13th August 1912, the day being ruled by Mars = 9 and its alternate Venus = 6, events were won by Lady Frederick II. = 3141

8254521222 = 42 = 6, Venus; Thimble Colt = 514235
2734 = 36 = 9, Mars; and Dennery = 4555521 = 27 = 9,
Mars.

Peculiar sequences of weights may also be noticed in connection with a series of events. Thus, in the first instance, 15th August, we get the following values :

2.0	winning weight	9·1	=1
2.30	,,	,,	8·9	=8
3.0	,,	,,	7·2	=9
3.30	,,	,,	9·8	=8
4.0	,,	,,	8·9	=8
4.30	,,	,,	7·10	=8

Here the values are those of the Sun and Saturn, with a single interloping of Mars in the third event. The 12th August, as given above, shows the following curious coincidence :

2.0	won by weight	8·11	=1
2.30	,,	,,	8·2	=1
3.0	,,	,,	7·12	=1
3.30	,,	,,	8·9	=8
4.0	,,	,,	8·7	=6
4.30	,,	,,	7·8	=6

Four of the events were won by the numbers 1 and 8, Sun and Saturn. On the following day there was an alternation of Sun and Moon numbers :

2.0	won by weight	8·11	=1	Sun
2.30	,,	,,	9·7	=7	Moon
3.0	,,	,,	8·5	=4	Sun
3.30	,,	,,	8·12	=2	Moon

On the 12th, at Folkestone, the values were:
8·11 = 1, 8·11 = 1, 7·9 = 7, 8·11 = 1, 7·11 = 9, 8·5 = 4;
four Sun numbers out of five events. Possibly
some patient research along these lines would
reveal an underlying law. I do not propose to
suggest one here, but merely bring the cases forward
as curious and interesting. As it may be anticipated that some of my readers will take a hint from
this, I may here give a tabular view of the weights
ruled by each of the planets according to their
numerical procession.

TABLE OF WEIGHTS

Planet.	Weights controlled by Planets.
Saturn . .	8·13, 8·4, 7·9, 7·0, 6·5, 5·10.
Jupiter . .	8·8, 7·13, 7·4, 6·9, 6·0.
Mars . .	9·0, 8·5, 7·10, 7·1, 6·6, 5·11.
Sun . . .	8·6, 7·11, 7·2, 6·7, 5·12.
Venus . .	8·11, 8·2, 7·7, 6·12, 6·3.
Mercury . .	8·10, 8·1, 7·6, 6·11, 6·2.
Moon . .	8·12, 8·3, 7·8, 6·13, 6·4, 5·9.
Sun . . .	8·9, 8·0, 7·5, 6·10, 6·1.
Moon . .	8·7, 7·12, 7·3, 6·8, 5·13.

By means of this Table the weights controlled
by the dominant planet can be seen, and the competitors carrying those weights are those which

alone have the winning chances, selection being made by triangulation of the values involved. Thus : Lincoln Handicap, 1912. Dominant planet Saturn = weights 8·13 Mercutio, 8·4 Long Set, 7·9 Moscato, 7·0 Cinderello, 6·5 Ben Alder, 5·10 Warfare —weights involved 9·6–6·1. The triangulation brings out the weights 8·4 and 7·3, and Long Set, the nearest to 8·4, won, while Uncle Pat, 7·3, was second, Warfare being third. Our planetary weight would therefore have taken us directly to Long Set when triangulated.

At 3.10 on Thursday, 28th March, at Liverpool, the Spring Cup was won by Subterranean. The dominant planet was again Saturn, and among his weights we have already found 7·0, which was the weight carried by the winner of this event. The frequency with which this gravity of the planets, as determined by their respective numbers, is carried out by events is really surprising, and deserves attention. It illustrates more forcibly and conclusively than anything else could do the existence of a law of numerical ratios, a geometry which encompasses both gravity and planetary velocities. It informs us once more that the force of gravitation is inversely as the velocity of the body attracted. Thus, we see that a body moving at a tangent to the line of attraction can only overcome gravity by its velocity. If it had no motion it would be immediately impelled along the line of attraction directly to the centre ; but, in proportion as it has velocity, it is able to overcome attraction. We overcome the gravity of

the earth by motion. When the propelling force
of a body in flight is stayed, the body slows down,
expends its velocity, and eventually falls to earth.
The velocities of the planets being in proportion to
their distances, they come under a law of numerical
ratios. Consequently, any study of their connection with events must be founded upon their
primary cosmic relations. It is by the observation
of the coincidence of an event with its theoretical
cause that we are able eventually to formulate a
law. We may do this either by a number of direct
observations all pointing to the same cause, or we
may adopt the method of exhaustion, and by a
process of exclusion bring ourselves at last to
recognise the operative factor. Thus, if a given
event can be examined in regard to the position or
cosmic order of each of the planets in succession,
we shall eventually arrive at the conclusion that
such event can only be attributable to a particular
planet, and a number of observations can then be
made to establish this conclusion.

By taking the direction and force of the wind at
any seaboard, and working in connection with the
tidal constants, we may, after a series of observations, predict the time and height of the tide with
great accuracy. The constant factor here is M–S,
or the Moon's distance from the Sun. Wind
pressure is a variable factor which has to be taken
into account. Similarly, we may say that at a
certain point of time the same factors may apply
to the weights carried by competitors or to the
gravity-value of certain numbers, or colours,

because these latter have a gravity-value on account of their being definite vibrations, and vibration is always in terms of velocity. Suppose, now, that we say M–S=D, then it will be found the weight will depend on S+D, or S–D, where S is the horary equivalent. This is so uniformly the case that it puts the question of chance entirely out of the field. Consequently, when estimating the chances of a given event falling to a definite selection, we only employ the doctrine of probabilities in default of any certain knowledge of a Law of Values; but in knowledge of this law we wisely drop the word "chance" out of our vocabulary. It is found that every competition, no matter how many competitors may engage, can be reduced so as to divide the winning chance between two, and this will yield the winner in 80 out of every 100 events. This surely puts the case beyond doubt.

It has been suggested that the same principles might be applied to lottery numbers, and some investigations into this matter have yielded curious results. For the purpose of illustrating a successful method of dealing with lotteries, I shall have recourse to a further exposition of the "Secret Progression" (*Kab.*, i. p. 67 *et seq.*).

Having obtained the five numbers of the last drawing of the lottery, they must be set down in a line, and reduced by consecutive subtraction (adding 90 when necessary, as there are 90 numbers in the drawing), and thus a second line of numbers will be obtained, which, being similarly dealt with, will yield a third line of numbers, and these again will yield a fourth line, each line being reduced by one number, and in the result we obtain one final number.

Example.—The five numbers drawn for prizes at the Rome lottery on 6th January 1894 were 63, 48, 60, 27, and 81. These we deal with for the first reduction to obtain the Mother Number, thus:

```
63
48   75
     12   27
60        45   18
     57        42   24
27        87
81   54
```

The Mother Number is therefore 24. This composed of 2 tens and 4 units. We deal with the tens first of all.

Place the tens on a line to the left, with the digits following in usual sequence, until three lines are formed. Thus:

2	3	4
5	6	7
8	9	1

Here 2 is the figure representing the tens in 24, and therefore it holds the first place, and is followed by 3 4 5 6 7 8 9, when it is seen that one space remains in the square for 1, which is the completion of the series.

Now deal with the units, placing the units of Mother Number in the first square:

24	3 –	4 –
5 –	6 –	7 –
8 –	9 –	1 –

The second units are obtained by adding 5 to the units of the Mother Number, curtailed by 9, if necessary. Thus, the units of the Mother Number are 4, to which add 5, and obtain 9, which are accordingly the units of the second tens, making 39. To 9 add $5 = 14 - 9 = 5$, and we have the units of the third tens. So continue until the full series is completed, when the square will appear thus:

24	39	45
51	66	72
87	93	18

The next step is to couple the numbers, adding them together and deducting 90 wherever they amount to more than that number. The result exhibits six numbers, thus:

$$24+39=63 \qquad 84=39+45$$

$$51+66=27 \qquad 48=66+72$$

$$87+93=90 \qquad 21=93+18$$

Finally, these are coupled again, and we have three numbers, thus :

$$63+84=147-90=57$$
$$27+48=\ 75 \qquad 75$$
$$90+21=\ 21 \qquad 21$$

The three numbers, or "Daughters" of the Mother Number, are therefore

57,   75,   21,

and these are to be followed on five consecutive occasions, that is to say, at the five drawings following upon that of the 6th January 1894, from which we took our numbers for the extraction of the "Mother."

The following were the drawings referred to :

13th January	44— 1—63— 5—25	Lost.
20th ,,	37— 9—39—21—1	Won 4th.
27th ,,	80—57—15—14—69	Won 2nd.
3rd February	80—83— 4—19—78	Lost.
10th ,,	57—76—59—81—74	Won 1st.

Hence the stake of $15=5$ times 3 will yield $42-15=27$ gain.

The Italians have many methods of dealing with these chances, the most usual being the Pyramid. For this they take the numbers extracted at the last drawing. The drawings take place weekly, and there are always five winning numbers. These they set down and reduce to unit value :

$$44-1-63-5-25$$

$$8-1-\ 9-5-\ 7$$
$$8-1-\ 9-5-\ 7$$
$$7-2-\ 9-1-\ '5$$

$$5-4-\ 9-2-\ 1$$

The unit values being doubled and added together, throwing out the nines as formed, the figures 7, 2, 9, 1, 5 result ; and these are added again to the two rows above, throwing out the nines, so that the figures 5, 4, 9, 2, 1 are obtained. These are written from left to right and repeated from right to left, using the last figure 1 as the turning point :

$$5\ 4\ 9\ 2\ 1\ 2\ 9\ 4\ 5,$$

which gives us the base of the Pyramid. The Pyramid is built up by pairing the numbers and throwing out the nines, thus :

$$
\begin{array}{ccccccccc}
5 & 4 & 9 & 2 & 1 & 2 & 9 & 4 & 5 \\
 & 9 & 4 & 2 & 3 & 3 & 2 & 4 & 9 \\
 & & 4 & 6 & 5 & 6 & 5 & 6 & 4 \\
 & & & 1 & 2 & 2 & 2 & 2 & 1 \\
\end{array}
$$

until the fourth row is reached, when selection is made by taking the two numbers to the left and the

10

two to the right, which here are 12 and 21, which are accordingly selected as the numbers to be followed in the next drawing.

The numbers 44—1—63—5—25 were drawn at Rome on 13th January 1894, and these, as shown, yield 12 or 21. Accordingly, the winning numbers on the 20th January were 37—9—39—21—1. As these include one of the numbers selected, the result is satisfactory. As the curious reader may wish to test the value of the method for himself, I here give the actual figures drawn for January 1894:

6th January	63—48—60—27—81
13th ,,	44— 1—63— 5—25
20th ,,	37— 9—39—21— 1
27th ,,	80—57—15—14—69

I may now give a further key to the resolution of numerical chances which will serve for lotteries.

The five numbers extracted for the first drawing each month are taken as the basis of the calculation, and serve for the remaining three weeks of the same month.

1. Reduce the numbers to their unit values. To the first add 3, to the second add 1, to the third add 4, to the fourth add 1, and to the fifth add 5. Now, compose the numbers to the total, and also their unit values. Reserve the last number, *i.e.* the total of the unit values.

2. Proceed again in the same way to add 1 to the first extraction of the month, 4 to the second, 1 to the third, 5 to the fourth, and 3 to the fifth.

3. To the same numbers add successively 4, 1, 5, 3, 1.

4. Add 1, 5, 3, 1, 4 to the same numbers.

5. Add 5, 3, 1, 4, 1 to the same numbers.

You will now have 5 totals of whole numbers and 5 totals of unit values. It will be seen that the unit value totals afford two numbers. Add these together to obtain the third.

These three numbers must be followed for the remaining three drawings of the same month.

Example.—6th January 1894, Rome. Numbers drawn—63, 48, 60, 27, 81.

1. Reduce to unit values:

	63 = 9	48 = 3	60 = 6	27 = 9	81 = 9
Add	3	1	4	1	5
Total	12	4	10	10	14 = 50
Unit	3	4	1	1	5 = 14
2.	9	3	6	9	9
	1	4	1	5	3
	10	7	7	14	12 = 50
	1	7	7	5	3 = 23
3.	9	3	6	9	9
	4	1	5	3	1
	13	4	11	12	10 = 50
	4	4	2	3	1 14

4.	9	3	6	9	9
	1	5	3	1	4
	10	8	9	10	13 = 50
	1	8	9	1	4 = 23

5.	9	3	6	9	9
	5	3	1	4	1
	14	6	7	13	10 = 50
	5	6	7	4	1 = 23

Our unit totals are 14, 23, which, being added, yield 37. These three numbers are to be followed for the drawings of 13th, 20th, and 27th January 1894. Results:

        13th January   44- 1-63- 5-25
        20th   „   37- 9-39-21- 1
        27th   „   80-57-15-14-69

Observe also:

        14 = 5
        23 = 5
        ———
        37 = 10 = 1 came out twice.

If to the sum of the unit values of the numbers drawn you add 14, the result will always be the sum of the unit values of the resolution. As—

$$9\text{—}3\text{—}6\text{—}9\text{—}9 = 36$$
$$\text{Add} \quad 14$$
$$\overline{}$$
$$50 = 5$$

Chance number $14 = 5$

„   „ $23 = 5$

The numbers drawn for the 3rd February 1894 were 80, 83, 4, 19, 78.

Reduced to unit values:

$$8\text{—}2\text{—}4\text{—}1\text{—}6 = 21$$
$$\text{Add} \quad 14$$
$$\overline{}$$
$$35$$

This number 35, when resolved by its five circular parts, 31415, yields the Chance Numbers 17 and 26, which, being added together, give 43. Hence the numbers 17, 26, and 43 are to be followed for the next three drawings.   Result:

10th February	57-76-59-81-74
17th „	68-17-42-57-31
24th „	43-79- 8-13-25

Here, again, the lowest and the highest of the Chance Numbers came out according to the rule.

When the total of the unit values is also the sum of the numbers plus 14, the numbers must be reversed, and the number 14 will be a winning one. Thus, on 3rd March 1894, 30, 19, 37, 35, 73 being drawn, the unit values are:

$$3—1—1—8—1 = 14$$
$$\text{Add}\quad 14$$
$$\overline{}$$
$$28$$

But $3—1—1—8—1$
Plus $3—1—4—1—5$

$$\overline{}$$

$$6—2—5—9—6 = 28$$

which is the unit value total.

But $3—1—1—8—1$
Plus $1—4—1—5—3$

$$\overline{}$$

$$4—5—2—13—4 = 28$$
and $4—5—2—\ 4—4 = 19$
$$\overline{}$$
$$47$$

Therefore 47 becomes 74, and 14 will be our other number, being a multiple of 28.

Result of the subsequent drawings :

10th March   22-**74**-44-43-81
17th   „   36-68-**14**-25-57
24th   „   72-**14**-36- 2-40
31st   „   62- 6-**14**-78-26

Here our numbers come out no less than four times in as many drawings.

This kabala is not invariable, but has a basis in fact which renders it extremely valuable. The following is the paradigm.

The digits 0 1 2 3 4 5 6 7 8 9 = 45, and 4+5 = 9. Therefore 9 is the basis of the unit value of all numbers and the key to the mensuration of all chances. The value $3 \cdot 1415 = 14$, and is the expression of the relation of the circumference of a circle to the diameter of the same. A nearer expression is $3 \cdot 14159$ (*Kab.*, i. p. 13).

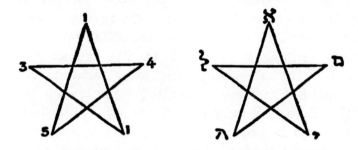

Pico della Mirandola wrote on the subject and gave a table of sympathetic numbers showing what numbers answered to those drawn, and hence were likely to be drawn in sequence. These I have tested very severely, and I condemn them utterly. It is hardly likely that a man who was known as " the scourge of astrology " should be capable of divining upon so subtle a matter.

A more reasonable method is that of the progress suggested by Benincasa. It consists in pairing numbers which have a major probability of turning up in a sequence. Thus :

81 and 72, 53 and 16, 25 and 50, 87 and 84, 59 and 28, 22 and 44, 84 and 78, 56 and 22, etc.

Applied to the year 1894, I find a stake of 1 wins 13, a stake of 45 wins 81, another stake of 45 wins

81, in the course of 19 drawings; which shows a
net gain of 84, or at the rate of about 4½ for each
drawing. This, however, is mere "betting to
figures," and any such progressive system will
yield commensurate results. My object is not to
formulate a system, but to show affinity of numbers
and the working of a law of numerical ratios in
matters ordinarily relegated to the domain of
Chance. This can always and most certainly be
done, but not in a book intended for public circulation. Here it is only possible to give hints that
are valuable in proportion to the intelligence and
interest of the reader. One such is contained in a
very astute statement by one of the old writers,
who uses the pentagon in much the same way as I
have used the pentacle. His key numbers are 7,
29, and 34. He arranges the five numbers last
drawn at the five points of the pentagon, and
successively adds together A B C, B A D, C A D,
D C B, and multiplying the sum by E, and also
dividing, he gets three numbers which may be used
either singly or in a combination for the next
drawing.

A similar idea is contained in the cross of numbers
said to be appropriate to each month of the year.
Thus, for January they have :

$$1$$
$$3 \quad 4 \quad 2$$
$$4$$

To these are attached certain cryptic verses, and
concerning the above it says, in the last line of the

quatrain : " Dieci volte il destro ed una al lato "
—" Ten times the right and one to the side."
The right-hand number being 2, the value is
$10 \times 2 + 1 = 21$.

In addition to this, we have the numbers 14, 44,
41, 34, and a reasonable degree of success marks
the proceeding when compared with the records.
Thus, in January 1894, we have drawn 44, 21, 14 ;
in January 1895, 44 ; in January 1896, 44 ; in
January 1897, 34 and 41. But it would be quite
impossible to follow all the combinations of the
Cross of Numbers through the four drawings in
each month with hope of ultimate advantage.
The only possible means outside of the Secret
Progression, which is a kabalistic expression of the
cyclic law in numerical sequences, by which one
may determine the forthcoming numbers in a lottery,
is by reference to their gravities, as indicated by
the horary equivalents of the disposing factors at
the time of the drawing, and this method is not to
be understood by those who have had no prepara-
tion in astronomical studies. Sufficient, however,
has been said in this place to indicate the existence
of a numerical sequence by which we may argue
from coincidence to law.

CHAPTER X

SOME NEW VALUES

THE general experience of uncertainty which pervades the question of planetary periods and the mode of their reckoning, together with the yet more doubtful problem of phonetic values, has induced me to give the matter some attention. It will be convenient if in this place I indicate, for the benefit of those who have not ploughed through my *Cosmic Symbolism*, what are the points at issue.

It was the ancient astrological practice in India to count time from sunrise, and it persists to this day. Obviously, in the state of astronomical science among the populace of India, nothing but approximations could be expected. But the jyoshis and others skilled in the mathematics of the subject were, and are, capable of giving the time of apparent sunrise with great accuracy. That is to say, they could determine the apparent longitude of the Sun at any time by means of their astronomical tables, and could calculate the time at which this longitude would be on the celestial horizon of any locality. They then divided the day into 60

hours of 24 mins. each, counting from sunrise as
we count from noon. Approximately, there would
be 5 ghatikas, or 120 mins., for the rising of each
complete sign of the zodiac, or 4 mins. for each
degree, and hence a person born so many *ghatikas*
and *vighatikas* (hours and mins.) after sunrise could
be informed from the position of the Sun in the
zodiac at the time of its rising under what degree of
the zodiac he was born. But the chronometry of
the ancient astrologers was very faulty, and the
sun-dial was perhaps the most accurate means of
measuring time known to them. They had no mean
or true clock-time. But nevertheless they divided
the signs into 30 parts called *trims'âmshas*, and
allowed 4 mins. for each of these parts. They
gave the same names to the days of the week as
do we, and they recognised the same zodiacal order
of the signs and the same planetary rulerships
in those signs. European astrologers later gave
attention to the subdivision of the day, and intro-
duced what are called " planetary hours." The
planetary hour is one-twelfth of the time between
sunrise and sunset. Now, in equatorial parts,
this would be almost uniformly 12 hours, but in
northern latitudes the length of the day would
vary according to the season of the year.

Hence the doubt has arisen as to whether the
hour should be a secular one of 60 mins. or a planetary one of one-twelfth the diurnal arc of the Sun.
My own view is that, counted from sunrise, the
hours should measure of equal length from sunrise
to sunset, six of such hours being included between

sunrise and noon, and six between noon and sunset.
The mistake some astrologers have made is that
they have counted the hours from midnight,
making a blend of secular and astronomical meas-
ures, thereby overlapping noon by some minutes
instead of completing an hour exactly at the four
cardinal points of the local circle of observation.

Further, the vexed question of phonetic values
in the matter of coding has given rise to serious
misgiving in the minds of those who have followed
the rules given in some misleading works by
amateur exponents. I have only one view on this
point, and it is that every letter which contributes
to the sounding of a word or name, and especially
if such be in a stress syllable, must be counted.
In such a name as Calliope the *i* is not only long,
but forms the stress syllabus, and to omit it would
be sufficient reason for omitting anything. I
always use it (*Kab.*, i. p. 30), and its value is 1.

Some other values not included in my Table of
Phonetic Values (*Kab.*, i. p. 30) will be found in my
Cosmic Symbolism.

The object, therefore, should be to find a method
which, while satisfying the law of values, leaves no
doubt as to the planetary period involved. Such a
method I have discovered. It is based on the old
view that the day begins at noon and not sunrise.
That the first hour after noon is ruled by the planet
giving its name to the day, and is followed by the
others in Chaldean order (according to apparent
velocities), and every hour is of equal length, viz.
sixty minutes. Then it will be necessary to take

note of the day planet, the hour planet, and the period planet.

The day includes 24 hours of 60 minutes. The hour includes 15 periods of 4 minutes. The first hour after noon is ruled by the day planet. All periods count from the day planet. Here, then, is the

Table of Periods

Noon to 7 p.m.

Planet.	Day.	Periods.						
☉	Sunday .	12☉	1♀	2☿	3☽	4♄	5♃	6♂
☽	Monday .	☽	♄	♃	♂	☉	♀	☿
♂	Tuesday .	♂	☉	♀	☿	☽	♄	♃
☿	Wednesday	☿	☽	♄	♃	♂	☉	♀
♃	Thursday .	♃	♂	☉	♀	☿	☽	♄
♀	Friday .	♀	☿	☽	♄	♃	♂	☉
♄	Saturday .	♄	♃	♂	☉	♀	☿	☽
Signs of Zodiac .		♑♒	♐♓	♏♈	♌	♎♉	♍♊	♋

This will be sufficient for purposes of a demonstration. It will be seen that the planets read from left to right in the Chaldean order, as on Saturday: Saturn, Jupiter, Mars, Sun, Venus, Mercury, Moon—these being according to the apparent velocities of the several bodies as seen from the earth. The slowest is given the first place.

Suppose I want the period ruling on Friday at 3 p.m. Under the figure 3 and in a line with

Friday I find Saturn. Therefore Saturn begins to rule at 3 o'clock, and will continue for 1 hour. The first 4 minutes, from 3.0 to 3.4, will be ruled by ♀. Hence it is a Venus period in the hour of Saturn. To enumerate this we take

$$
\begin{array}{lll}
\text{Day planet} & ♀ & =6 \\
\text{Hour} \quad \text{,,} & ♄ & =8 \\
\text{Period} \text{,,} & ♀ & =6 \\
\hline
& 20 & =2
\end{array}
$$

Therefore among a number of contestants the Moon should win, but if not present by name-value the sign the Moon is in must be taken. Thus, suppose the ☽ not represented by a 2 or 7 among the competitors ; then by looking in the Ephemeris we find the ☽ on that day in the sign ♈, and our Table shows that sign at the foot of the planetary periods immediately under ♂, and so Mars is the planet which disposes of the Moon or in whose " House " the Moon is that day. Hence, in default of 2 or 7, we look for 9. Some examples will serve for the purpose of clearing up any doubts in the matter and making the whole plan clear to the reader.

Plumpton, 5th January 1912. Day, Friday = 6.

Hour, 1.15—Mercury 5—Per. ♄ = 8.
$$658 = 19 = 10 = 1, \text{ negative } 8.$$
Phyllis, $836 = 17 = 8$ won.

1.45—Mercury 5—Per. Jupiter 3.

    653 = 14 = 5.

    Volauvent, 66366252 = 36 = 9 won.

2.15—Moon 2—Per. Saturn 8.

    628 = 16 = 7.

    Bridge, 223 = 7 won.

2.45—Moon 2—Per. Jupiter 3.

    623 = 11 = 2.

    Mint Tower, 454 462 = 25 = 7 won.

3.15—Saturn 8—Per. Saturn 8.

    688 = 22 = 4.

    Place Taker, 8316 41212 = 28 = 1 won.

3.40—Saturn 8—Per. Saturn 8.

    688 = 22 = 4.

    Wavelass, 616316 = 23 = 5 won.

Here it will be seen that five out of six events are
straightforwardly accounted for by phonetic values
of the competitors, taking the periods of the planets
in the order stated above. It will be noticed that
Volauvent, a French name, is phonetically vŏlōvŏng
= 66366252 = 36 = 9.

The alternates here used are :

Saturn	8—1	Sun.
Venus	6—3	Jupiter.
Mercury	5—9	Mars.

The Moon is taken as of value 2 in this case,
being negative to Saturn and Jupiter. In the
periods of Venus, however, it is positive. As to
Wavelass, the winner of the last event, it was well

indicated by symbolism of the Moon, ruler of the ascending sign Cancer, being exactly on the cusp of the second House (finance) and in good aspect to Uranus, Mars, and Venus, and conjoined with Neptune. Here Cancer and Neptune rule the ocean wave, and the Moon is that lass that loves— or loveth not—a sailor, according to its fickle whim.

Take another place on the same day:

5th January 1912, Haydock Park.   Friday = 6.

1.0 —Mercury 5—Per. Venus 6.
  656 = 17 = 8.
  Claydon, 231425 = 17 = 8 won.

1.30—Mercury 5—Per. Venus 6.
  656 = 17 = 8.
  Lady Scholar, 3141 62232 = 24 = 6 won.

2.0 —Moon 7—Per. Venus 6.
  676 = 19 = 1.
  Climax, 231412 = 13 = 4 won.

2.30—Moon 7—Per. Venus 6.
  676 = 19 = 1.
  Calliope, 2131681 = 22 = 4 won.

3.0—Saturn 8—Per. ♀ 6.
  686 = 20 = 2.
  Jacobus, 312626 = 20 = 2 won.

3.30—Saturn 8—Per ♀ 6.
  686 = 20 = 2.
  Great Peter, 2214 81412 = 25 = 7 won.

Here, again, we have five out of six events clearly in harmony with the law of phonetic values and the

periodicity of the planets.   I cannot say if in the
1.30 event there was no 8 or 1 present, but I observe
that, in any case, Saturn 8 was on that day in the
sign of Venus 6, and that 6 won.   This would only
be allowable in default of 8, when of course it
would be quite regular and what we should expect
by the rule.

The next day at Plumpton affords further indications of the general reliability of this very simple
method.

6th January 1912.   Saturday = 8.

1.15—Jupiter 3—Per. Sun 1.
$$831 = 12 = 3.$$
Beauty Bird, $2641224 = 21 = 3$ won.

1.45—Jupiter 3—Per. Venus 6.
$$836 = 17 = 8.$$
Penitent, $8154154 = 28 = 1$ won.

2.15—Mars 9—Per. Sun 1.
$$891 = 18 = 9.$$
Saucepan, $62685 = 27 = 9$ won.

2.45—Mars 9—Per. Venus 6.
$$896 = 23 = 5.$$
Early Closing, $1231\ 236752 = 32 = 5$ won.

3.15—Sun 1—Per. Sun 1.
$$811 = 10 = 1.$$
Campamento, $2148141546 = 36 = 9$ won.

3.40—Sun 1—Per. Sun 1.
$$811 = 10 = 1.$$
Snap, $6518 = 20 = 2$ won.

All but the last two events are in line with the

principles laid down in this new theorem. It will be seen that we have held rigidly to the positive values of the planets except in the case of the Moon when operating in combination with a masculine or positive planet, such as Saturn, Jupiter, and Mars. Also it will be seen that the values of the sounds are those given in Part I. of the *Kabala of Numbers*. The whole name is used in every case. Only the schedule or set time of the event is employed, no allowance being made for a speculative "off" time. Finally, we employ all the factors, namely, the day, hour, and period planets, and the combination of the positive values of these three factors gives us 14 out of 18 events in harmony with the rules.

I will take only one more example and complete the illustration with events at Haydock Park on the same day, namely :

6th January 1912.   Saturday = 8.

1.0—Jupiter 3—Per. Saturn 8.
           838 = 19 = 1.
           Barnet Fair, 212514 812 = 26 = 8 won.
1.30—Jupiter 3—Per. Saturn 8.
           838 = 19 = 1.
           Shaun Aboo, 325 126 = 19 = 1 won.
2.0—Mars 9—Per. Saturn 8.
           898 = 25 = 7.
           Blunderbuss, 2325412226 = 29 = 2 won.
2.30—Mars 9—Per. Saturn 8.
           898 = 25 = 7.
           Borough Marsh, 2264123 = 20 = 2 won.

3.0—Sun 1—Per. Saturn 8.

       818 = 17 = 8.

       Bembridge, 214223 = 14 = 5 won.

3.30—Sun 1—Per. Saturn 8.

       818 = 17 = 8.

       Ilston, 13645 = 19 = 1 won.

Here, again, are five out of six events in accord with our simplex system. I do not think it is necessary to labour the point further. Had there been any doubt as to the values attaching to the various sounds, or if the rules for determining the planetary period in force were at all vague, then some might claim an adventitious display of proofs. But all our values are contained in previous works, *Kabala I.*, *Cosmic Symbolism*, etc., and the only new element is the introduction of the most ancient method of time divisions. One may reasonably be in doubt as to what constitutes local sunrise, but nobody can have two minds about clock time at Greenwich. The question may be asked, what allowance is to be made for E. and W. longitude ? The answer is, none at all so long as the events are timed by Greenwich. Probably the reason for this will be found in the fact that cosmic influences are distributed through centres, as, for example, in the case of planetary influence in national affairs being paramount in the horoscopes of kings. The world is governed and also timed from centres which are focal depositories of latent cosmic forces. But we cannot argue beyond facts, and these clearly show that Greenwich time serves

for all events that are timed by the clock in the
limits of this country.

Here, then, are nineteen out of twenty-four events
in direct succession, bearing out the values ascribed
to the planets, the phonetic values of names, and the
alternate values of the various periods. This high
record of 79 per cent. is altogether beyond the limit
of a fortuitous coincidence, and hence we must
conclude that our evaluations are valid, and that our
rediscovery of the ancient system of time-division
is upheld by the facts.

I have purposely chosen events of popular interest
because they are on record and can be checked
in every detail. It would have been possible
to extend this survey indefinitely, and I have
some months of consecutive records on hand.
I am not, however, writing a book on Turf
Uncertainties, but merely stating a theorem, viz.
that the day begins at noon, and I am here giving
a kabalistic proof that it is so.

Obviously, any system that employs name-values
is comparatively useless, for the reason that there
will most frequently be one or more competitors
whose name-values are of equal unit significance,
i.e. of the same or alternate values, as Velca, Remiss,
Sfax, Lady Senseless, all in the same event won by
Sfax. In short, a method of exclusion has no
practical value, and only a scientific method of
selection is at all worthy of consideration. It can
be shown that a definite method of selection based
on the gravity-values of the three factors, and
supported by the laws of Tycho and Ptolemy in

regard to cosmic interaction, is a scientific fact
that has been under rigid test for years past, and
the average percentage of such tests is not less
than 75 continuously.

It may be of use for the testing of this method of
Planetary Periods if I here give a Table of the values
for every half-hour during the week from noon to
six o'clock.

Time.	12.0	12.30	1.0	1.30	2.0	2.30	3.0	3.30	4.0	4.30	5.0	5.30
Sunday .	2	2	7	7	6	6	8	8	9	9	4	4
Monday .	5	5	6	6	1	1	7	7	8	8	4	4
Tuesday .	9	9	1	1	6	6	5	5	7	7	8	8
Wednesday .	1	1	3	3	4	4	8	8	5	5	6	6
Thursday .	6	6	3	3	4	4	9	9	8	8	1	1
Friday .	3	3	2	2	4	4	5	5	9	9	6	6
Saturday .	7	7	2	2	8	8	9	9	5	5	4	4

These values are for the day and hour planets
combined, and the times indicate the beginning of
their influence. To these values must be added
the number of the period planet.

Rule.—Divide the minutes after the complete
hour by 4. The product will give the period planet
counted from the day ruler.

Example.—On Tuesday, what rules at 2.35 p.m. ?
$35 \div 4 = 9$. Counted from Mars (Tuesday) we
arrive at Sun = 1. Then 2.0 = 6 and 2.35 = 6 + 1 or 7.

The idea that man may compass a fortuitous
fortune by the application of numerical systems to
the chance events of life is by no means an extra-
ordinary one. It is by means of a mensuration of

the various subtle forces in Nature that man has
been able to avail himself of them in his daily life ;
and chemistry, among other of the sciences, only
began to be properly studied when it was allied
to mathematics. So far as the world in general
knows anything at all about the action of the
luminaries upon mundane affairs, the belief is that
the Sun is the source of light and heat, and that it
exerts a gravitational pull upon all the planetary
bodies, including the Moon and Earth. It is further
believed that the Moon is the chief cause of the tides,
and that it has some vague traditional associations
with lunacy. It is known to reflect light. Not
everybody knows that it also reflects heat, or that
of the light rays it reflects some are converted into
heat rays by the earth's atmosphere. But who gave
out that light, heat, and gravitation were the only
forces exerted by the luminaries, or that the planets
exerted none at all of their own ? We cannot
accuse the ancients of this exclusiveness. They
fully recognised that each of the planets transmitted
the vital energy of the cosmic heart in varied forms.
They affirmed that the rays of Mars were irritant,
that those of Venus were soothing, that Jupiter
augmented the vital forces and Saturn diminished
them. Thales believed that the universe was made
from water, a fluid base. Doubtless he was led to
this belief by the fact that water crystallises at
an angle of 60°, and that this angle has first importance in the mensuration of a circle. It was
observed, too, that planets at an angle of 60° or 120°
affected one another in a manner which was not

the case at 59° or 61°, at 119° or 121°. It has always been our fault that we have regarded the ancients as necessarily more ignorant than ourselves. As a matter of fact, however, it will be found that as to essential facts they knew as much as ourselves —I think they knew very much more,—and that only in the matter of more accurate observation we have excelled them by the use of modern instruments. Modern science has not even arrived at the conclusion that Saturn has any influence at all upon other bodies of the system, still less on human life. Ignoring the prime postulate of the solidarity of the solar system, the interaction of the planetary bodies plays no part in modern science. The idea that everything exists for use is not adequate excuse for a scientific interest in these remote bodies of the system, and, placed as they are at thousands of millions of miles from the Sun about which they revolve, they are regarded as barren wildernesses upon which no conceivable humanity can exist. And yet if they are held by the force of gravitation, the light, heat, and vital energy of the Sun must also reach them. It is rather a sorry case that men of science know so much about the microscopic germs of disease and nothing at all about a planet that is more than a thousand times larger than the Earth, and whose rays have probably more to do with pathology than all the bacteria that were ever isolated and classified. Of course, all this about planetary influence may be a mere superstition, but that does not prevent us from making a science of it by noting coincidences. The idea that the Moon has something to do with the tides may be a superstition, but it does not hinder us from noting the coincidence of its elongation with the daily recession of the time of high - water. Science is not concerned with causes, but with the tabulation and comparison of facts.   Hence we may evade the philosophical consideration of causes and apply ourselves solely to the task of noting the coincidences between sound, number, and planetary velocities, and thereby establish what we may call the science of phonetic values, of numerology, and of planetary symbolism.   It may well serve as a working hypothesis for a very much wider view of cosmic and human relations than has yet been adopted.

CHAPTER XI

COLOUR VALUES

So far we have been dealing principally with numbers and their significance in human affairs. It has been suggested that Sound and Colour have their numerical relations. So far as Sound is concerned we have, I think, consistently shown that phonetic values are linked up with planetary influence, or at least that there is a correspondence between the unit value of a name and the planet which, in the Chaldean scheme of astronomy, answers to a particular time when that unit value is conspicuous. We may now deal with Colour values.

According to the scheme already propounded, the planets are each related to one of the primary or prismatic colours. In this scheme

Violet	is related to Jupiter.
Indigo	,, ,, Saturn.
Blue	,, ,, Venus.
Green	,, ,, Earth's satellite.
Yellow	,, ,, Mercury.
Orange	,, ,, Sun.
Red	,, ,, Mars.

In this scheme Venus denotes the Intuitive or Spiritual Intellect and Mercury the Rational or Material Intellect. They are united temporarily

in earth-life, indicated by the Earth (for which the
Moon stands proxy) and the colour Green. The
permanent union of the lower and higher phases
of the mind, through the experience of incarnation,
is an amalgam which, according to the Hermetic
Philosophers, changes copper into pure gold. In
all these philosophical speculations we find that
mercury is the active principle. It stands for
experience, and when this is properly digested in
the " egg philosophical " and united to copper, the
mercury is entirely absorbed and the copper is
changed to gold. The philosophers speak of the
perfect man as Hermaphrodite, that is to say, a
permanent blend of the two natures, Hermes =
Mercury, and Aphrodite = Venus.

Changing our theme we may change our colours,
and find them thus related to numbers : Violet = 3,
Indigo = 8, Blue = 6, Green = 7, Yellow = 5, Orange
= 1, and Red = 9.

Arranging the digits in their numerical order,

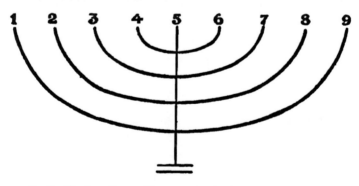

we find that when the opposites are united from
either end we get the unit value of 1 ; as 1 + 9 = 10

$=1$, $2+8=10=1$, $3+7=10=1$, $4+6=10=1$, and
the unpaired number is 5. Now, 1 is the *ens* or
vital principle in man, energy in the cosmos; and
5 is the experience principle in man, intelligence in
the cosmos. These two principles of life and consciousness answer to the gold and mercury of the
alchemists; the desirable thing and the means of its
attainment. Mercury 5, therefore, was regarded as
the universal solvent. Its symbol is compounded
of the Circle, the Crescent, and the Cross, the three
great religion symbols of the world. Hermetically,
they stand for the Spirit, Soul, and Body, the Sun,
Moon, and Earth, and are comprehended only in
Mercury, the principle of consciousness. But when,
by means of the "Red Dragon," the planet Mars,
the number 9, which are symbols of the Will, the
ens had been incorporated with the quicksilver $=$
Mercury, then we might look for the realisation of our
quest in the production of the material gold. Thus:

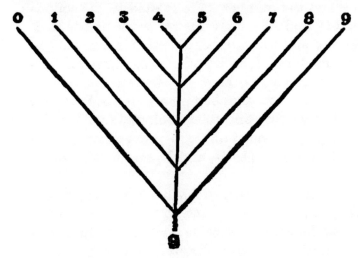

Intelligence therefore arises from experience, and is the only true solvent of our problems. By intelligence, impelled by the power of the will, the *magnum opus*, or great work, can alone be brought to a satisfactory conclusion. When, therefore, we seek to bring our speculations to a satisfactory conclusion, we must make prime use of experience.

Now, we have seen that certain numbers or unit values of sounds answer to planets, and therefore to colours, for Sound, Number, and Colour are bound up together in the universal expression of the Law of Vibrations.

Saturn and the number 8 are thus related to all sibilant sounds, such as S, Sh, and Z. They answer to the colour Indigo.

Jupiter and the number 3 are related to all palatals, as Ch, J, and soft G. They correspond with Violet.

Mars and the number 9 are related to the sounds K, hard G, and R. They answer to the colour Red.

The Sun and the numbers 1 and 4 are related to the sounds A and I, and to the colour Orange; also the consonants M, D, T.

Venus and the number 6 are related to the vowels O and UW, and to the colour Blue.

Mercury and the number 5 are related to the sounds E, the aspirate H, and N, and to the colour Yellow.

The Moon has relation to the numbers 7 and 2, and to the labials B, P, F, V, and to the colour Green.

It may be said that some writers fix the correspondence of letters and planetary numbers entirely

by their numerical values : thus Saturn, whose
number is 8, is said to govern all letters whose
phonetic value is 8, as Ch (guttural), Ph, P ; Jupiter,
whose number is 3, would thus govern the letters
or sounds G (soft), L, Sh ; and so of the rest. But
to this arrangement experience offers some excep-
tions, especially regarding initials.

Returning now to our colours, we have found that
there is a gamut of colour as well as a gamut of
sound and number related to the planets. In
order to make a test of the colour values it will be
necessary to introduce some elements of astrology.
A figure of the heavens being set for the time and
place of an event in which contestants may be
known from their colours, it will be found that three
specific points or parts of the heavens will give a
clear indication of the dominant or winning colour.
In the case of the Wars of the Roses, we had but
to decide between the relative strength of the red
and the white, *i.e.* Mars or the Moon. But in a
mixed field, where the colours represent a financial
as well as a sporting interest, the variety may be
so great as to require some discrimination. It will
be found then that the body colour which is
dominant is that chiefly to be regarded. The head
or cap is related to the first House, which corresponds with the sign Aries, and is that section of
the heavens immediately below the horizon of the
East. The body colour, which is the principal one,
is determined by the fifth House, the part of the
heavens which is from 120° to 150° from the East
horizon, and which corresponds to the sign Leo.

These Houses, of themselves, answer to the colours White and Gold; but when occupied by any sign they take the colour of that sign, which is determined by its ruling planet. Thus, if Saturn were in the fifth House at the time, we must look for Indigo or Black to win, or if Capricorn were there it would be the same, because Capricorn is ruled by Saturn. If Mars were just rising, or the sign Aries was on the East horizon, a red cap would fit the winner very well indeed.

So, according to the signs and planets occupying the fifth and first Houses, we judge of the body and cap colours of the winning competitor. But if a single planet be conspicuous in the heavens, either by its exact rising, culmination, or setting at the time, or by its being in elevation in its own sign, then that planet will give its note of colour, to the exclusion of all others. In this connection it should be noted that the Moon, when in a watery sign—Cancer, Scorpio, or Pisces—shows green; but in other signs it shows straw colour, pale yellow, or cream. The colours of the planets are variously:

Neptune—Lavender, lilac, heliotrope.
Uranus—Stripes, grey, black and white.
Saturn—Indigo, dark blue, black, or chocolate.
Jupiter—Violet, purple.
Mars—Red, scarlet, crimson.
Sun—Gold, orange.
Venus—Primrose, turquoise, pale blue.
Mercury—Yellow, sometimes pink.

Some useful examples of the working of this

colour scheme in matters of selection will be found in *The Silver Key*.[1]

Let us now examine the working influence of colour in daily life. Red is perhaps the most striking colour it is possible for a man or woman to wear. It immediately arrests attention, and generally excites comment. The pathological effects of colour must have been noted by the publisher who first blazed into public notice by using red covers for the display of his books. Red is an irritant to all but Martians, and to them green probably means the same thing as does red to us Terranians. The pathology and psychology of colour are things to be noted in daily life. Green has a soothing effect, as all know who have lived long upon the sandy plains of the tropics. It conveys a sense of refreshment and acts as an anodyne. The red hair of the true Martian is always accompanied by the steel-grey eye : " An eye like Mars to threaten and command." Soldiers whose regimentals are red attract general notice—too much so in action,—and " one drunken soldier damns the army " because of this conspicuous colour. The rank and file are getting a better reputation since they went into khaki. We never imagine how much influence colour exerts upon us until we study it in a critical manner. We are affected by scenery without understanding art ; we are moved by melody without a knowledge of music ; and, similarly, we are influenced by colour without any idea of what chromopathy may mean.

[1] Foulsham & Co., London.

The young lover who is scrupulous about the setting of his cravat has a fancy for colour, the science of which altogether escapes him. Neither does he know that the colour of his cravat, the carpet on which he stands, and the wall-paper which forms a background to his figure, have quite as much to do with the success of his campaign as any undiscovered traits of character of which he may imagine himself to be possessed.

Black, which is defined as the absence of colour, arises naturally from the privation of light, either radial or reflected. It is universally associated with evil and death. Its influence is depressing, and the pathology of colour has been so far apprehended by the poets that they uniformly picture despair as black. Disaster has produced a " Black Monday," disease has made " the Black Death " famous throughout Europe, and what are known as " the Black Assizes " are so characterised by reason of the outbreak of jail-fever. What was formerly known as Merrie England has been transformed into Melancholy England since Puritan methods obtained in regard to dress. But, according to *The Tailor* and the *Fashion Book*, we are beginning to wake up and find that life has some joy and colour in it.

Purple and gold belong to royalty, because they are the colours of Jupiter and the Sun, the two greatest bodies of our system and the symbols of opulence and grandeur. The Order of Melkizedec arose from the association of Jupiter (Zadok) with the priestly kings, and they are represented as clothed in purple.

The fire and energy of Mars is well expressed in the properties of the colours red, crimson, and scarlet. It is the planet of Freedom, answering to the number 9. The Red Cap, or *Bonnet Rouge*, of the Revolutionists is the Cap of Liberty, or shall we say, in this case, of licence. In its sinister aspect Mars is the symbol of carnage, fire, and the sword. Its conjunctions with Saturn (symbol of Death) in the various signs of the zodiac have been seen to coincide with bloodshed and carnage either by international or civil war in those countries ruled by such signs (*Kab.*, i. 78–80). In 1792 Mars was stationary in the sign Virgo, ruling Paris, and in that year the Revolutionaries established the Republic. In the cyclic revolution of the universal horoscope the present age comes up under the dominion of the sign Aries, ruled by Mars. Consequently it has been called the Iron Age, because steel and iron belong to Mars by tradition and to the great cosmical artificer Vulcan. After the Iron Age is the Copper Age, then the Age of Amalgams, then the Silver Age, and, lastly, the Golden Age. These are under the dominion of Venus, Mercury, the Moon and Sun respectively.

Blue is akin to green in that it acts as an anodyne. It is a true nervine, and restores the equilibrium of the nerves produced by the effects of light and activity. Consequently it symbolises Peace, Purity, Truth, and Grace. It is the vesture colour of the Madonna in combination with white.

Yellow is a laxative colour and acts as a purgative, like mercurous chloride. It corresponds to the

12

stage between disease and health when Nature is
putting off effete tissue and impurities of all kinds.
It also responds to the state of Purgatory, which is
that between the worlds of Death and Life, of
earth and heaven.   In medical practice it is customary after disease to employ purgatives before
administering tonics.   Mercury, as related to the
colour yellow, is also the cosmic symbol of experience, which is the means used by the Spirit to
purge the mind of errors and delusions.   We do
not therefore need to subscribe entirely to the
verdict of Solomon that this world's experience is
" vanity and vexation of spirit."   Vexation of
spirit it may be ; but it is not in vain, since it forms
a natural and necessary part of the process of
evolution.

Red is a stimulant and tonic, and purple increases
blood - pressure ;   black, brown, and indigo are
depressants.   The mental atmosphere of the pessi-
mist is brown, and even black ; that of the philosopher and deep thinker is indigo.   Indigo is
intensified blue, the deep well of truth into which
the speculative soul gazes when contemplating
universal problems.

If any doubt exists as to the actual influence of
colour on the human system, it is only necessary
to take a number of coloured glasses—red, yellow,
and blue,—fill them with pure distilled water, and
expose them for twenty-four hours to the sun's rays.
It will be found in effect that if the contents of the
red glass are taken on an empty stomach they will
act as a tonic, those of the yellow glass as a purga-

tive, and those of the blue glass as a nerve tonic,
of particular use in neuritis. By combining the red
and yellow, the red and blue, the blue and yellow
in equal proportions a variety of effects will be
observed. Temperature rapidly decreases under
a combination of the yellow and blue waters.
Anybody experimenting along these lines will be
convinced of the chemic action of light upon water
through coloured media. In New York there was
established some years ago a hospital for fevers, in
one ward of which all the smallpox cases were
treated. The window-glass of this ward was of a
red colour, and none of the cases showed any
"pitting." Prof. Babitt and Dr Albertini have
written extensively on the pathological effects of
colour, and have adduced numerous instances of
cases successfully treated. In acute cases of
neuritis and mania the use of "all-blue" surround-
ings has repeatedly proved to be efficacious. A
correspondent informs me that he has repeatedly
dreamed of persons dressed in grey, and in
every case they have met with accidents immediately afterwards. I have personal experience
to the same effect. It is obviously Uranus at work.

These remarks refer to the pathological effects of
colour. In material affairs the colours appear to be
transmitted through a coarser medium than the
astral body, for we repeatedly find that Mercury
(yellow) is represented by the Moon, that Mercury
takes up pink as if it were tinctured by Mars. On
the other hand, green is often represented by the
Moon in certain zodiacal positions.

These things being duly observed, it will be possible to institute a chromoscopic science in regard to matters in which colour variations are apparently of significance. Patrons of sport appear not altogether indifferent to the influence of colour, and "owner's colours" have before now been consulted in regard to speculations of this kind with commendable success. One system presents a colour for each House, another for each sign, and a third for each planet. But sometimes, as I have shown, all the colour is in the name, as, for example, Rubio = red, White Knight = white in red sign, Cream of the Sky = yellow in green sign, Grey Barbarian = grey (black and white) in white sign. The colours attaching to the Houses will be found in *Cosmic Symbolism*. Those of the planets are already known, and will be found in *The Manual of Astrology*. The sign colours are Aries, red; Taurus, pale blue ; Gemini, yellow ; Cancer, green ; Leo, orange ; Virgo, dark green ; Libra, pale yellow; Scorpio, black ; Sagittarius, purple ; Capricorn, white ; Aquarius, blue ; Pisces, grey.

Many of these colours are modified by the amount of light they reflect. Thus Pisces is a shining grey or pearl grey, not a dead ash colour. The green of Cancer is a shining green ; that of Virgo a dead green. I have also found that Scorpio is sometimes related to a deep blood-red, the colour of the car-buncle, as contrasted with the red of Aries, which is bright red like a ruby. Here it would seem that there is a red which is equivalent to black, and that both are related to the sign Scorpio. From some

experience in this direction of colour significance,
I have not the slightest doubt that a consistent
study of winning colours in relation to dominant
planetary influence would lead to an orderly
science of chromoscopy which could be profitably
followed out.

CHAPTER XII

PHRENOSCOPY

IT is not usual for the common-sense man, the spinner and toiler in the workaday world, to reflect upon his relationship to the universe of which he is an integral part. It is exceptional that he should consider anything of greater importance for the moment than the man who elbows him in the street or those with whom he is immediately concerned in business. But merely because he does not reflect upon this relationship of himself to his greater environment, does not alter the fact in itself. He is, nilly willy, an integral part of the great universe around him, and, all unconscious though he may be of the sources from which he is impelled to think and act, they nevertheless continue, without interruption, to influence him in every decision of his life, every project of his conception, every undertaking in which he may engage.

Man thinks himself independent of his environment, and able at all times to act with perfect freedom. This is the conceit and vanity of human nature. It is not a fact. As long as man is dependent on the very air he breathes, the quarter whence the wind may blow, and the light and heat which stream towards this our earth from the central luminary of the world, so long is he physically bound to respond to his environment in terms of his own nature.

But man is not a body only. He is not even essentially a body. Rather is he a mind possessed of a body. And equally by his mind man is related to the greater world around him. By the incident of birth he is already endowed with a definite character, a number of specific tendencies; and these, being related to an environment already in existence, must constitute for him the sole means of relative expression by which he is known to the world for what he is. Except in the few very rare colourless and inept characters which one may meet in the course of a long experience, it will be found that everyone is possessed of some dominant characteristic which enters into the expression of his nature in every single act of life. He has some dominant passion which controls his actions, shapes his ideals, and determines his attitude towards the world around him. He has some special aptitude which, unsuspected though it may be, finds illustration in every act of daily life. Seeing, then, that everyone has a predisposition, more or less strongly marked according to the inherent force of his nature, towards definite modes of thought and feeling and volition, we may inquire how he comes to be possessed of this individual accent; and how, being in possession of it, he can render it

purposive instead of automatic in expression;
consciously directing his powers towards definite
and predetermined ends, always following the line
of least resistance, which is ever that of greatest
progress, instead of blundering through the world
half his time trying to find a place that fits him
and one that he himself can fill.

The human brain, or that part of it which we
employ in the process of thinking, is a congeries of
minute cells which collectively constitute a species
of galvanic battery, which is capable of gener-
ating waves of electrical energy, differing in intensity and in mode of vibration according to the basic
constitution of the mind itself, and the efficiency of
its instrument—the brain.   Brain-cell vibration is
at the root of every thought, every act, every effort
of the will.   The brain, as the root of the whole
nervous system, is endowed with the power of
affecting and of being affected ; and it is a matter
of daily experience that very few brains exactly
syntonise or show responsiveness to one another.
If two persons live together for any length of time
they become syntonised automatically, the more
powerful of the two bringing the brain of the other
down to the frequency and mode of vibration
proper to itself.   Thus they arrive at a sort of
understanding which is a tyranny of the mind on
the one side and a slavery on the other.   Occasionally, as by nature endowed, we find two persons
who are capable of entering into immediate sympathetic relationship, who understand one another
instinctively, so to speak, and are in such perfect

"rapport" as to be able to impress one another even at a distance. This is the mystery of telepathy—feeling at a distance—which has recently engaged the minds of those interested in the study of psychological phenomena and mental science. The sympathy exists in the dominant *mode* of vibration, not in its frequency alone, though this is necessarily syntonised where such telepathic communication is possible. It may be produced automatically, as by hypnotism and other means.

The dominant characteristic, the ruling passion, the special aptitude is ever that which controls the greater issues of life and renders the individual effective for good or evil in the world. For although the whole brain is not employed in any single operation of the mind, yet those parts of the brain which are the more active claim an allegiance and a support from all other parts, so that if acquisitiveness or money-making (avarice) be the dominant passion, even love will be subservient to it, and a "marriage of convenience" will follow. This is what phrenology would teach us. But we are not immediately concerned with it or its problems.

How do we come possessed of certain characteristics, certain dominant passions and special aptitudes ?

Some may say it is hereditary influence, atavism. In such case the natives of India, and other countries where the caste system prevails, and where the individual is thereby relegated to a particular sphere of work and to a particular grade of social life, should for that reason be a specialist. Emphatically, he is not. The Brahmin ryot is not an expert agricultur:st. He can learn in our colleges what his ancestors have never dreamed of nor taught him. The soldier (kshetrya) is not a specialist. He is better trained by our English officers than ever he was by his forebears, and better equipped for warfare in every direction. Even the ghariwan, or professional coachman, has never attempted the coach and four. Yet his fathers for generations before him were charioteers and ashvakovidhas (skilful horsemen). In such case, too, butchers and housewives would not unite to produce poets, nor would the homely farmer and his wife number among their progeny the reformer, the statesman, and the explorer. In everything except mere physical tendency the supposed law of heredity breaks down at every point, and is all but abandoned by scientific men. The evolution of the genius is not deducible from the laws of hereditary transmission as hitherto explained and understood.

The reason of individual variants, according to the science of Phrenoscopy, is this : Every person is endowed with a brain of a definite constitution ; but that which determines its development, and the mode of activity in its cells, is nothing else than the electrostatic condition of the earth's atmosphere which obtains at the moment of birth. In other words, the moment a child is born and assumes independent existence, his first bre ith puts him into sympathetic relationship with his environment,

and thenceforth his particular mode of brain
activity is determined. And by this circumstance
also he is rendered sympathetic or antipathetic to
others born under similar or diverse conditions.
But if we inquire what it is that controls the changes
in the electrostatic condition of the earth's atmosphere, we shall inevitably be led by the *principia*
of the Newtonian Philosophy to refer to those
bodies which, together with the earth, constitute
the Solar System—the Sun, the Moon, and the
seven planets.

Now, we are informed by the study of embryology
that the segmentation of the ovarian cell, the
microscopic world in which organic life is com-
menced, is cruciform. That is to say, the cell,
which consists of a wall enclosing a space, is first
of all bisected by a direct line or wall of matter,
and afterwards by another that is transverse to it.
We learn also from a study of the tides that the
attraction of the earth's mass is greatest when the
luminaries are acting along the same meridian, and
next when they are in quadrature; and further,
that the local influence of any celestial body is
greatest on the meridian and on the horizon of a
place. And since the meridian and horizon are
planes at right angles to one another, we are led
to the conclusion that there may be an analogy and
a correspondence between these two orders of fact,
the physiological and the astronomical. Experience shows this to be the case.

When at the moment of a birth the meridian or
horizon is occupied by any one of the nine celestial

bodies—when, in fact, the celestial influence is acting directly or transversely in regard to the place of birth, the individual then born is impressed with the particular kind of electrical energy generated from that planet in the earth's atmosphere. The nervous matter infilling the brain cells immediately takes up and becomes responsive to that particular mode of etheric vibration which is dominant at the moment of birth. But this does not hold good with respect to the whole of the cerebrum. There are definite tracts or areas which are naturally allocated to the functions of the different orders of faculty, and there is a certain interdependence between these parts of the brain by reason of which they are capable of affecting one another. It is here that Phrenoscopy comes into direct touch and conformity with the established principles of modern Phrenology. The following diagram shows at a glance the particular areas of the brain which are responsive to the action of the various planets.

Here it will be seen that the planet Mercury is related to the Intellectual faculties—perception, memory, comparison, reason, etc. Jupiter has influence over the Sympathetic group of faculties —benevolence, suavity, imitation, wit. Saturn governs the Devotional group, consisting of veneration, ideality, etc. Mars controls the Self-regarding faculties—execution, destructiveness, combativeness, self-defence. The Sun rules the Governing group — firmness, self-esteem, conscientiousness, love of approbation. Venus has relation to the Affectional group, comprising continuity, adhesive-

ness, friendship, and inhabitiveness; and the Moon
relates itself to the Instinctual group, common to
man and the lower animals, including conjugality,
amativeness, love of offspring, love of life.   Uranus
is related to the medulla and spinal cord, and
Neptune to the more interior parts and processes

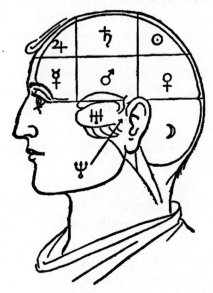

of the brain comprised in the pineal gland, the
pituitary body, and the corpora quadragemini.

Suppose, then, for the sake of illustration, that a
child is born when the influence of Venus is pre-
dominant, and the local mode of etheric vibration is
what may be termed Venusian.   That child will be
dominated in all the affairs of his life by the affections and those things which appeal to them or are
capable of stimulating that particular tract of
brain to which Venus is related.   But this is not

the whole of the matter, for it will be seen that, in order to dominate the thought, feeling, and action of life, the Venusian influence must have access, through the nervous matter of the brain, to every group of faculties located in, or functioning through, other tracts of the cerebrum.

Let it be supposed, for instance, that Venus was in the same line of position, or in the same part of the ecliptic, as the Moon at the moment of birth. Then, from what has already been said, it will follow that if Venus be the dominant influence it will act more strongly upon that group of faculties which are related to the Moon than upon any other group, producing, in effect, strongly marked affections and sensuous instincts. But if Venus were conjoined with Mercury, the affections would find a more intellectual expression, and the individual born under this influence would gravitate naturally in the direction of art, music, poetry, and the drama. Similarly, if Mars were the dominant influence at the moment of birth, and were conjoined with the Moon, the nature would be violent and destructive rather than executive and constructive. If acting in the same meridian or horizontal line with the Sun, the commanding and governing faculties would be stimulated and energised by the action of Mars towards the production of the soldier, the pioneer and explorer—the man in whom abundant energy and spirit are allied to a thirst for glory, mastery, and rulership.

Then, again, in accordance with this theory, which I claim to be invariably supported by facts, it becomes a matter of extreme interest and personal advantage to know what the dominant influence of one's nature may be, in what direction the natural powers will be most easily and effectively expressed, and in what particular line of life success will be assured.   The Key to this information is contained in the following

Phrenoscopic Chart

Neptune acts upon the mind of man to produce a highly-strung nervous temperament, often allied to either insanity or genius ; neurosis, aphasia, etc. It produces complications in business and an involved state of affairs generally.   Disposes to fraud, double-dealing, and irresponsible actions.   In the body it produces waste of tissue and a consumptive habit.

Uranus gives an eccentric mind, waywardness, originality, inventiveness.   Acting on the affairs of business, it produces sudden and unexpected developments, irregularities, rapid rise and fall, instability, unexpected turns of good and bad fortune. In the body it has relation to the nervous system, and its diseases are those of paralysis, lesion, and nervous derangement.

Saturn produces a thoughtful, sober, ponderable mind ; steadfastness, patience, and endurance ; disposition to routine and habit, method. In financial affairs it gives steady results commensurate with labour, success that is slow but sure, durance, hardships, privations. In the body it is related to the osseous system, and its ill effects are brought about by obstructions, chills, and inhibition of function.

Jupiter gives joviality, optimism, bountifulness, generosity, a rich and fruitful mind. It renders the subject fortunate in his affairs, giving success and frequently opulence. With this planet strong, a person never "goes under." In the body it has relation to the arterial process, and its diseases are those which arise from surfeit, congestion, and plethora.

Mars confers a sense of freedom, much ambition and executive ability, frankness, truthfulness, and scorn of consequence. It renders the mind forceful and militant, stimulates to new projects and enterprises, and in the body of man has relation to the muscular system. Its diseases are those which arise from inflammatory action in the tissues.

Venus confers poesy, good taste, fine feeling, artistic powers, gentleness, docility, dalliance, and love of pleasure. It renders the affairs pleasant and prosperous, giving profit from both artistic and rustic pursuits. Next to Jupiter it is the most benefic of the planets in its action on mankind. In the body it has relation to the venous system, and its diseases are those which arise from impurities of the blood, scorbutic and zymotic diseases, eczema, smallpox, measles, etc.

Mercury renders its subjects active, versatile, apt and business-like, disposed to much commerce, whether of the mind or the market, and eager in the pursuit of knowledge ; alert, and well-informed. Its influence on affairs of life is variable, for it always translates the nature of that planet to which at birth it is in nearest aspect. In the body it is related to the sensorium, the centres of sensation, and reflexly controls the nerves of action.

The Moon gives gracefulness of manner and suavity of speech, softness and adaptability of nature, variableness, love of change, romance, and adventure ; disposed to exploration and voyaging. In the body it corresponds to the glandular system, and its diseases are those incidental to the lymphatic glands and vascular tissue.

The Sun renders its subjects magnanimous, noble, proud, despising all mean and sordid actions ; loyal, truthful, and fearless. It produces honours and the favour of dignitaries, and renders the subject fortunate in the control of his affairs. In the body it controls the vital principle.

SUMMARY

	NORMAL.	ABNORMAL.
Neptune	Genius, inspiration.	Insanity, obsession.
Uranus	Originality, invention.	Obstinacy, eccentricity.
Saturn	Steadfastness, fidelity.	Deceitfulness, suspicion.
Jupiter	Benevolence, joviality.	Ostentation, profligacy.
Mars	Energy, executiveness.	Impulse, destructiveness.
Sun	Dignity, independence.	Vanity, egotism.
Venus	Affability, art.	Self-indulgence, disorderliness.
Mercury	Alertness, ingenuity.	Inquisitiveness, meddling.
Moon	Grace, idealism.	Inconstancy, awkwardness.

CHAPTER XIII

PLANETARY HOURS

HAVING shown that planetary hours count from noon in the most ancient system of time-division, it may now be of interest to learn of what use this knowledge is to us and how it can be turned to account in daily life.

For the sake of convenience to the reader I have here set out the numerical values of the twenty-four hours counted from noon of Sunday, which, by the same system, was always the first day of the week, as Saturday was the Sabbath (seventh) or last. To these values we have to add those due to the minutes past each hour. Thus we find that on Saturday at 2 p.m., which is the beginning of the third hour from noon, the value is 8, and if we want the value for 24 minutes past 2 o'clock, then we have to divide 24 by 4=6, and count to the sixth period from Saturn, which is Mercury=5, and by adding this to the day and hour value in the above Table, namely 8, we get 13, the unit value of which is 4. This responds to the negative Sun, the significance of which will be found in the following pages.

I. Table of Planetary Hours and Values

Hour.	Sun.	Mon.	Tues.	Wed.	Thur.	Frid.	Sat.
Noon	2	5	9	1	6	3	7
1 p.m.	7	6	1	3	3	2	2
2	6	1	6	4	4	4	8
3	8	7	5	8	9	5	9
4	9	8	7	5	8	9	5
5	4	4	8	6	1	6	4
6	1	3	3	2	2	7	6
7	2	5	9	1	6	3	7
8	7	6	1	3	3	2	2
9	6	1	6	4	4	4	8
10	8	7	5	8	9	5	9
11	9	8	7	5	8	9	5
12	4	4	8	6	1	6	4
13	1	3	3	2	2	7	6
14	2	5	9	1	6	3	7
15	7	6	1	3	3	2	2
16	6	1	6	4	4	4	8
17	8	7	5	8	9	5	9
18	9	8	7	5	8	9	5
19	4	4	8	6	1	6	4
20	1	3	3	2	2	7	6
21	2	5	9	1	6	3	7
22	7	6	1	3	3	2	2
23	6	1	6	4	4	4	8

Here follows the

II. TABLE OF HOUR DIVISIONS AND VALUES

Day.	4	8	12	16	20	24	28	32	36	40	44	48	52	56	60
Sun.	1	6	5	7	8	3	9	1	6	5	7	8	3	9	1
Mon.	7	8	3	9	1	6	5	7	8	3	9	1	6	5	7
Tues.	9	1	6	5	7	8	3	9	1	6	5	7	8	3	9
Wed.	5	7	8	3	9	1	6	5	7	8	3	9	1	6	5
Thurs.	3	9	1	6	5	7	8	3	9	1	6	5	7	8	3
Frid.	6	5	7	8	3	9	1	6	5	7	8	3	9	1	6
Sat.	8	3	9	1	6	5	7	8	3	9	1	6	5	7	8

The significance of the above Table is that it has to be employed in finding the value due to any number of minutes. Each hour is divided into 15 parts of 4 minutes each, counting from the planet which rules the day. Thus on a Saturday, ruled by Saturn, the whole day has the value of 8, and the hours count from noon, which is ruled by Saturn for one hour and is followed by Jupiter, Mars, etc. Then the value for each succeeding hour has to be added to the Day Planet's value, as shown in the first of these Tables.

The Period Planet is also counted from the Day Planet, as shown in the second Table, and its value is to be added to the value derived from the first Table.

Example.—What is the value for Tuesday, 2nd September 1913, at 5.25 in the afternoon ?

Table I. shows the hour from 5 to 6 p.m. to be ruled by 8
Table II. gives for 24–28 minutes on a Tuesday 8
                                                          ——
The total of these is . . . 16

Thus we obtain at once the unit value of 7, which
is the number of the Moon, and we therefore know
that the value 7 is ruling for 3 minutes after 5.25
p.m., and that it is under the direct or positive
influence of the Moon. Again, supposing that
the time given were 3.45 on Wednesday morning.
Let it be supposed that a child were born at
that time. It is required to know under what
number and Star it was born. According to
Table I. it is seen that Tuesday, at 15 hours
after noon, is under number 1, and Table II.
informs us that on a Tuesday 45 minutes after
the hour is under 5. Therefore we have 1 plus
5 equal 6, which is the number of the Nativity,
and hence the child would be born under the
planet Venus.

Supposing that there is a competition which
begins at a particular time, as, for instance, a race
of any description. By means of these Tables we
may at once decide upon the numerical value of
the winning competitor's name, or number if he
carries one. For in a very large majority of cases—
so large as to preclude the idea of a fortuitous
coincidence—it will be found that the planetary
value of the time of commencing the competition
or race will coincide with the value of the name of
competitor or the number he carries.

But it is found that the hours have a significance
which is dominant during their rule or sway, and
the use to which this can be put is in the selection
of the times for performing any work according to
its nature, and also a knowledge of the influence

of the ruling planet enables us to make forecast of the result of any effort, the contents of letters, the nature of messages, etc., that may be received under their rule.

For this purpose Table I. is alone to be used.

The influence and signification of the planets are as follows :

Planetary Indications

1. In the hour ruled by this number. Persons indicated by this number will be independent, proud, and magnanimous, scorning deception and meanness of every sort. They are bold and fearless, and capable of governing others and taking positions of trust and authority. Subject when ill to defects of the heart and circulation, and to hurts and diseases of the right eye.

Things sought for in this hour should be found in the East, and are brought to light at the full of the Moon.

Persons applying to one in this hour are ruddy, with grey or blue eyes and strong active bodies.

Letters received during this hour are relative to affairs of credit and position, honours, dignities, public persons, places of government, etc.

2. This hour is ruled by the Moon in its negative aspect, and is unfortunate, especially in regard to all matters having to do with females, changes, etc. Things lost will not be found. Persons applying are shifty and unreliable. Journeys are unfortunate. Letters refer to changes and misfortunes, and are often of the nature of evasion.

3. Ruled by Jupiter. A fortunate hour. Persons indicated by this planet are generous and even extravagant, disposed to help others, to their own detriment. Fond of good living and very grandiose in their ideas, pompous, but kind. They usually have full foreheads and protruding eyes, large teeth and plentiful hair, waving or curling, but in mature years they are disposed to baldness.

Things sought for in this hour may be recovered by searching in the N.-E. direction. If stolen, they will be restored if notice is given, with a reward.

Complaints to which the subject is predisposed are those of the liver and spleen, congestion and surfeit, sometimes flatulence.

It is a fortunate hour in which to avail oneself of legal advice, to consult churchmen, and to obtain favours from judges and magistrates. It is fortunate for all financial transactions and for general commerce, also for advancing one's interest in any direction. It is unfortunate for sailing or for dealing in cattle.

Letters received during this hour will have reference to money, trade, justice, and are always indicative of some advantage to the person receiving them. Information given at this time is reliable.

4. This number is ruled by the Sun, but is negative and unfortunate. Persons applying to one during this hour are haughty and proud, conceited and overbearing, fond of display and bigoted.

Things sought for in this hour are seldom recovered, but may be so at the New Moon if sought for in the N.-W.

Letters received relate to loss of position, defects of credit and esteem, and sometimes they are threatening and blatant.

The diseases of those born under this number are those of the blood, and generally arise from lack of tone or vitality.

It is an unfortunate hour in which to do anything of importance or to approach persons in authority, or to go a journey or enter a house for the first time.

5. Ruled by Mercury. Persons applying in this hour are usually tall and thin, but, if short, will be extremely wiry and active, and rather wizened in appearance. The eyes are small and sharp, and the appearance very alert and businesslike. The hands are slender, and the step quick and nimble.

Things lost generally prove to have been stolen, but they are usually recovered if sought for in a Northerly direction.

Messages received relate to writings and to papers, to business and trade, and to educational matters, books, and matters affecting young children. Sometimes to short journeys and to health.

The diseases of those born under this influence are chiefly nervous, affecting the brain and the organs of speech, and sometimes the limbs. Various forms of neuralgia, vertigo, brain sickness, pellagra, epilepsy, and defects of the senses and memory are the chief ailments of Mercury.

6. Ruled by Venus. Persons applying at this hour are of a kind, gentle, docile, and amiable disposition, disposed to the arts and culture of various forms. Sometimes easy-going and lovers

of pleasure, to their own hurt and detriment. The body is well favoured and fully fleshed, the limbs round and supple. The hair fine and of a light brown or flaxen colour, sometimes very black and abundant. The eyes may be either dark and sloe-like, or of a fine blue colour, as suits the complexion. Generally good-looking if male, and pretty if female, but always attractive.

The hour is good for all matters pertaining to the sexes and for the pursuit of things of beauty, fashion, and pleasure. It is good at this time to prefer a suit, and to become engaged or to marry. A good hour for domestic affairs and for entering a new home. Good for journeys and for taking trips, but not for setting out on a long voyage, and principally for matters of a domestic and social nature—visiting, shopping, calling on friends, etc.

Things lost in this hour are to be found in the West.

The diseases to which those born under Venus are subject are those arising from the morbid expression of the passions, sexual complaints, and diseases of the throat and kidneys ; skin diseases, phlebitis, etc.

Letters received at this time relate to pleasure and to domestic and social affairs, and sometimes to affections.

7. Ruled by the Moon. The person applying under this number is usually of full body, fleshy and pale, with rounded features and colourless complexion. Hands and feet small, head large. In character the individual is self-assertive and fond of praise.

The Moon governs all persons attached to public service. It denotes public bodies and Government or municipal servants.

Things lost or observed to be lost in this hour will be recovered if public notice is given of the fact. The thing should be looked for in the North, and will come to light in the full of the Moon.

The diseases to which those born under this influence are subject are chest affections, diseases and complaints of the stomach and breasts, bad digestion, injuries or bad defects of the left eye and the brain.

The hour is good for dealing with matrons and all public concerns, municipalities, affairs of public interest, journeys, voyages, changes of all sorts, advertising, etc.

Letters and messages at this time relate to journeys and changes, and there are female influences involved. The hour is good in contradistinction from the hour ruled by Moon under number 2.

Nevertheless it is best not to take any important steps under this influence, as changes of plan and arrangement are apt to intervene to spoil the best results. It is especially good for dealing with all matters affecting the public, and also public bodies of government.

8. This number is ruled by Saturn. It is an evil hour, and bad for almost all affairs, but singularly good for dealing in land and the produce of the earth—minerals, crops, etc.

Persons applying are usually of a dark and lean

visage, sinister in appearance, and stooping in gait. Hardly to be trusted, because selfish and material to a degree.

The hour is good only for dealing with the aged and infirm, and for matters connected with the produce of the soil, such as crops and minerals; but also for any matter in which time is a prominent factor, as in the case of contracts reaching over many years.

Things lost during the hour of Saturn are seldom if ever regained, but should be looked for in the South, and they may be found, but only after long delay.

Letters in this hour relate to death, sickness, misery, disease, misfortune, darkness, mourning, and delays.

It is not a good hour in which to deal with anything, as it shows delays, deceptions, treachery, and loss. The Hebrews made the whole day, so far as it related to business, a holiday and period of rest.

A person falling sick in this hour will have a long period of illness, and will only recover after much care and expense. Mental impressions received during this hour should be carefully thought over before being acted upon, as they are generally faulty.

The diseases of Saturn are those of the bones and articulations, morbid decay, consumption, melancholia, and religious mania.

9. This number is ruled by Mars. Persons applying during this hour are such as have a sandy or ruddy complexion and grey, steely eyes. They

are usually strong and muscular and very militant in their manner. It is better to placate them than to oppose. They are petulant and fiery and very impulsive, yet frank and outspoken, and easily dealt with on that account alone. You know what they mean and intend to do as soon as they speak.

Things that are lost in this hour are usually found almost at once or not at all. They are to be sought for in the West.

The diseases of Mars are those that are incident to the head and face, and also the excretory system. Fevers, accidents, and affections of the skin; itchings, swellings, and blains; cuts, burns, scalds, and corrosions.

Letters received during this hour are such as relate to disputes, frauds, thefts, lying, fire, accidents, fevers, operations, and tragedies.

Do not trust news that is received or impressions that come to the brain during this hour; do nothing hurriedly, but test all communications and act deliberately after mature thought.

The above indications are useful in regulating one's affairs and making decision in matters that are productive of doubt in the mind. The ancients paid great attention to these Elections, as they were called, and seldom did any work of importance without regard to the current influences as expressed in the hour of the day.

Some writers have used the Planetary Hours as beginning at midnight in a conventional manner not at all known to the ancients, while others have

used them as from the time of sunrise, always
omitting to say what is meant by that very ambiguous term. Sunrise may be upon the local
horizon or upon the celestial horizon, and may be
apparent or true sunrise. If sunrise is to be taken
at all, it should be taken astronomically, that is to
say, by the conjunction of the Sun's apparent
centre with the celestial horizon of the place for
which calculation is made.

I have found that the ancient method of using
the hours is in close agreement with the events of
daily life, and for that reason alone have adhered
to it in practice. Elsewhere in the pages of this
work I have given examples of the manner in
which the evaluation of names by the Phonetic
alphabet brings them into accord with the value
of the Day, Hour, and Period involved, and these
examples will be sufficient proof of the integrity of
the system. We have now to consider one or two
propositions of a more recondite nature connected
with the subject of planetary influence in human
life, and these will suitably conclude the second
part of the Kabala.

CHAPTER XIV

SCIENCE AND SUPERSTITION

In the foregoing pages we have seen that there is a Law of Values attaching to Form, Sound, Number, and to all expressions of the universal vibration of the etheric agent. It has been demonstrated in other places that the planets deflect and transmit the Solar rays in altered magnetic and electrical conditions, differing as does the nature of the planet transmitting them. Those who are disposed to regard the conclusions of astrology as fanciful and inconsequent should reflect on the fact that the planet Mercury is second to none in importance among the spheres, which would certainly not be the case had the ancients judged by appearances only and not by experience and reason. Here we have a planet which is about 22,500 times smaller than Jupiter, and so near at times to the Sun as to be seldom visible; indeed, I believe I am right in saying that the great astronomer Copernicus confessed never to have seen it. Yet this planet above all others is taken to be the specific significator of man, inasmuch as it is related by astrology to the intellectual and reasoning faculties as distinguished from the emotional and passional common to man and the lower animals.   With thinking people this fact will weigh very heavily, and in the scientific mind it may serve to remove the prejudice which has long existed against the science on account of immature presentation and frequent misrepresentation at the hands of critics who are wholly ignorant of the subject.

It is a matter of considerable satisfaction to me to know that Mr George F. Chambers, F.R.A.S., in his admirable little work, *The Story of Eclipses*, has admitted that there is *prima facie* evidence for scientific inquiry into the connection between eclipses and earthquakes.   He says : " Perhaps this may be a convenient place to make a note of what seems to be a fact, partly established, at any-rate, even if not wholly established, namely, that there seems some connection between eclipses of the Sun and earthquakes.   A German physicist named Ginzel has found a score of coincidences between solar eclipses and earthquakes in California in the years between 1850 and 1888 inclusive.   Of course, there were eclipses without earthquakes and earthquakes without eclipses, but twenty coincidences in thirty-eight years seems suggestive."

Had Ginzel taken the trouble to extend his observations beyond California, and to include eclipses of the Moon as well as those of the Sun, and further, had he taken note of planetary transits over the places of eclipse, his coincidences would have been considerably amplified.   The fact is that you cannot get the average astronomer to

recognise the working value of the fundamental
concept of Newton's *Principia*, that of the solidarity
of the Solar System. Beyond the fact of planetary
perturbation caused by the interaction of the large
bodies of the system they do not care to inquire
whether there may not be other forces than the
attraction of gravitation at work in the system.
In this they err very greatly. It was by the
recognition of the law of planetary interaction as
implied by the concept of the solidarity of the
system that Laplace discovered the great perturbation of Saturn by the planet Jupiter, and paved
the way to the discovery of Uranus by Herschel,
the discovery of which was a unique performance
in the history of astronomy.

Sir David Brewster was more catholic in his
ideas, and fully admitted that if the Sun's rays were
necessary for the development of chromatic effect
and the faculty of vision, there may be other rays
which enable us to hear, to taste, and to smell.
I would go further and say, without any reserve
whatsoever, that there are rays, more subtle than
those of light, more far-reaching than the force of
gravity, which impel men to think and to act,
which create disasters, produce various forms of
sickness, inspire ambitions, and dispose men to
definite lines of conduct. And I say this with as
much authority and from as weighty an experience
as any which at any time has been adduced in
support of a scientific proposition. In line with
me are such men as the astronomers Tycho, Kepler,
Newton, Wichell, Wing, Flamsteed, and Christie;

the writers Sir Thomas Browne, Dryden, Varley,
and Garnett, and a host of others whose names and
works have embellished the records of antiquity.

In these pages I have not advanced any one of
the more weighty arguments, nor adduced any part
of the voluminous body of proofs which might be
urged in favour of an *astrologia sana* such as that
to which Bacon subscribed, for it has been my
express purpose to entertain the popular mind
with such material as can legitimately be advanced
as a part of the Kabala. Incidentally, however,
this matter goes to prove that there is a definite
law of correlation at work in the universe, and that,
whether we regard the cosmic as embodied Force
or merely as a symbol of Mind, it submits equally
to an orderly and systematic interpretation.

I have purposely refrained indeed from making
any specific references to the scientific and philosophical value of astrology as a system of interpretation. This is not from want of any material,
but from lack of space in which to deal fairly with
it. But yet I have felt that there is a subtle
connection between numerology and the various
branches of kabalism, and astrology, which renders
the development of the one almost impossible
without the introduction of the other. Certainly,
without a knowledge of astrology one cannot go
very far in kabalism, and I think that symbolism of
any sort, whether it be religious, Masonic, Rosicrucian, or pure Art, cannot go far without coming
into direct relations with astrology.

For purely forensic purposes it may be conveni-

14

ent to regard all celestial configurations as merely symbolical. It is a somewhat difficult matter, apart from the introduction of a species of occultism, to argue a connection between the presence of Mars in a particular degree of the zodiac and a blood temperature of 105°, between the passage of Uranus over the place held by the Moon at a birth and the presence of the subject in a motor smash-up, or between the transit of Venus over the place of the Sun at birth and the marriage of the person at an age exactly corresponding to the interval of time between the birth and the transit at the rate of a day for a year. Yet these are among the common observations of the student of astrology. If, however, we regard the planets as symbols, the argument rests solely in the correspondence of symbol and event, and the man who would talk them out of existence must inevitably fail.

In seeking for purely physical connections between earthquakes and eclipses, we may consider the fact that the lifting power of the Moon over all fluidic nature is exceedingly great, so great indeed as to raise millions of tons of water several feet in the course of a few hours. There are various means by which this may be effected, and the popular view is that it is caused by the attraction of the Moon upon the particles of water composing the ocean. When the Sun and Moon are conjoined, and both pulling in the same direction, we have what are called Spring Tides, when the effect is greatest. When pulling from opposite sides of the earth, the same bodies produce Neap Tides, when

the effect is not so great.   Now it is known that the
period from one high tide to the next is 12 hours
25 minutes, and this interval comprises a half
revolution of the earth on its axis plus the 25
minutes represented by the meridian passage of the
Moon's elongation (increase of Moon's longitude over
the Sun's) during the interval.   We are able therefore to link up the tides with the Moon's elongation
and to define the joint action of the luminaries as
greatest at conjunction.   But all conjunctions of
the Sun and Moon are not eclipses of the Sun, the
reason being that the Moon's path does not lie in
the same plane as that of the earth, and consequently crosses it at an angle, which is found to be
about 5°.   The point of intersection is called the
node, and it is only when the luminaries are conjoined on, or close to, this node that there can be
an eclipse of the Sun.   They are then pulling in a
right line together on the same side of the earth,
and the visible effect is that the sun's rays are cut
off from the earth in that region where the eclipse
is central at noon, that is to say, where the centres
of the Sun and Moon appear to coincide when they
are exactly on the meridian.   At the eclipse of the
Sun on 12th April 1912, and in other cases, the fall
of temperature at the moment of greatest obscuration was such as to be a matter of general comment.
What would be the effect of this sudden disturbance
of the temperature ?   Obviously there would be an
immediate uprush of heat from the interior parts
of the earth to counteract the chill and to restore
the equilibrium.   Further, the electrostatic con-

dition of the atmosphere would undergo a sudden change, and a similar outburst of electrical energy would be required to compensate it. The earth's crust at this part of the globe may or may not be strong enough to withstand the strain, and the effect is in the latter case a violent earthquake shock. Consequently we only look for violent earthquakes at or immediately after the time of an eclipse in those parts that are volcanic, or within what are known as the earthquake areas. Similar effects, due entirely to the strain set up between the contending forces of the Sun and Moon, may be observed at an eclipse of the Moon. In the case of the solar eclipse we have the interposition of the actual body of the Moon, whereas in a lunar eclipse it is only the shadow of the earth that is the cause of obscuration. In this connection it appears to me essential to the purposes of physicists that the static effects of solar and lunar eclipses should be carefully observed before we can argue much concerning the nature of the forces that are impeded in either case. But it may be remarked that such study and observation will inevitably lead to a re-modelling of our ideas regarding the nature of the forces transmitted by the luminaries. For whereas it is generally conceded that the Sun is the source of all light and heat, and that the Moon merely reflects these, it would seem that the effects of lunar eclipses are just as conspicuous as those due to solar eclipses. Ricciolus has observations of earthquakes following both eclipses of the Sun and Moon, and Morrison in recent times made similar

observations and records. In one instance, at all
events—that of the Cumana earthquake,—he specifically predicted and located the disturbance. It
does not appear to have arrested scientific attention,
however, and probably because at that date no
scientific authority had argued a connection between earthquakes and eclipses. It is well to keep
these facts warm, however, for it is commonly
observed that the folly of to-day is the science of
to-morrow. A hundred years ago you could not
photograph a body through a brick wall, or fly in
the air, or communicate with a person a thousand
miles away in a few minutes; nor, for that matter,
could you predict the time and place of an eclipse
with any certainty, and, with the exception of the
latter, any talk of doing these things would have
been a " sure sign " of enfeebled intellect.

When, therefore, we hear people talk of the folly
of planetary influence in human life, which is the
description of what astrology imports to us, we get
impatient, first because they are inconsistent, and
next because they are presumptuous in pretending
a knowledge they do not possess. For, beyond
all human cavil and controversy, there is the fact
that we are creatures of the Earth; the further fact
that the Earth is an integral part of the Solar
System; and, moreover, the fact that every atom
exerts a direct influence on every other atom
throughout the system to which it belongs. When,
therefore, we are asked to believe that cosmical
conditions, at a time when the Sun, Mars, Jupiter,
and the Earth are all in the same line, are exactly

the same as when these bodies were not so placed,
we are entitled to conclude either that Newton was
a great dreamer or the speaker a greater fool.   We
prefer the latter conclusion as more in harmony
with our estimate of the facts.   Elsewhere I have
proved that the periodic times of the planets
Mercury, Venus, Earth, Mars, and Jupiter, when
taken together, average exactly to the periodicity
of sunspot maxima; and Sir Norman Lockyer has
shown a connection to exist between maximum
sunspot periods and high Nile tides, droughts, and
other physical phenomena, so that, by purely
scientific means, we are coming to the point where
it will be not only possible but only rational to
argue a connection between the planets and mankind.   For a long time it may be called " physics "
or " physical astronomy," but when it gets its
right name, that under which it has survived the
ages in face of all the ridicule and persecution of
the sceptic and the tyrant, it will be known as
Astrology, the science which, in the opinion of
Newton, was committed to primeval man by direct
revelation, since by no other means could he account
for its great antiquity and the universality of its
principles.   I doubt not that the astrology of
Newton was of that rational kind to which modern
science is steadily approaching, but what he knew
of it was grounded in the traditions, incorporated
in the *Tetrabiblos* of Ptolemy, and confirmed from
experience by Kepler.   To such studies we may
profitably apply ourselves without, at this day, in-
curring either much ridicule or much persecution,

and in this connection the present effort may be of service as showing the existence of many curious coincidences which can hardly be accounted for except on the grounds of a universal physiognomy, a symbolism that touches all phases of human experience and vaguely approaches the cusp of science. In connection with it we have been able to trace the Law of Vibrations, that of Periodicity, and the relations of both to matters of common human interest. A kabalism that is so inclusive can hardly lay claim to be considered in the light of a science, but it leads directly to the study of the problems of science which we have touched upon in this chapter, and perchance it may extend to that region of Higher Physics which pertains to the science of Mind. That it is not wholly without interest is sufficient excuse for its publication. If it should also be found to have a use, so much the better for the patient reader, to whom my thanks are due.

CPSIA information can be obtained at www.ICGtesting.com
Printed in the USA
LVOW11s1446101015

457765LV00001BA/160/P

9 781585 093373